Blinding Moment

Studies in Austrian Literature, Culture and Thought

Translation Series

General Editors:

Jorun B. Johns
Richard H. Lawson

Gert Jonke

Blinding Moment

Four Pieces about Composers

Translated and with an Afterword

by

Vincent Kling

Ariadne Press
Riverside, CA

Ariadne Press would like to express its appreciation to the Bundesministerium für Unterricht, Kunst und Kultur for assistance in publishing this book.

.KUNST

Translated from the German:
Der Kopf des Georg Friedrich Händel
Sanftwut oder Der Ohrenmaschinist
Geblendeter Augenblick: Anton Weberns Tod
© 2001 Jung und Jung Verlag, Salzburg
Catalogue d'oiseaux
© 2002 kolik (October 2002)

Library of Congress Cataloging-in-Publication Data

Jonke, Gert., 1946-
  [Geblendeter Augenblick. English]
  Blinding moment : four pieces about composers / Gert Jonke ; translated and with an afterword by Vincent Kling.
      p.   cm. -- (Studies in Austrian literature, culture, and thought. Translation series)
  ISBN 978-1-57241-156-2 (alk. paper)
1. Messiaen, Olivier, 1908-1992. Catalogue d'oiseaux—Poetry. 2. Handel, George Frideric, 1685-1759—Fiction. 3. Beethoven, Ludwig van, 1770-1827—Drama.
4. Webern, Anton, 1883-1945—Fiction. I. Kling, Vincent, 1942- II. Title.
  PT2670.O5G3513 2008
  830.8'03578--dc22

                                                          2008009657

Cover Design
Beth A. Steffel
Drawing: Andreas J. Fischbacher

Gert Jonke

Photo: Ingrid Ahrer
Courtesy Jung und Jung Verlag, Salzburg

Contents

THE HEAD OF GEORGE FREDERICK HANDEL

In many regions of the world there exists the custom of burning away winter on the first night of spring with enormous bonfires atop the highest mountains and hills of the countryside. This was the latest point, belief had it, at which the last of the snowflakes would go swirling around with a rain of pulverized ash from the woods, often set ablaze in this way.

In 1748 the Treaty of Aix-la-Chapelle was celebrated by burning away war. Better times were to be inaugurated with a magnificent fireworks display. They erected the most massive building they could for the pyrotechnicians to allow them to launch their burning pictures up into the night sky with all the greater daring. And, so as to allow the fire of his music worthily to accompany the many-colored, blazing images in the firmament, they assembled for Handel the largest orchestra that supposedly had existed up to that time.

Twelve thousand people had turned out for this event, most of them on foot. Unfortunately, however, the building just constructed must still not have been massive enough, for when, at the height of the festivities, the whole thing exploded and burnt down, causing a disastrous panic to break out, Handel might well have been one of the few to whom it occurred that the last of the dead from the war now burned away were also the first of the dead from the new peace that had already taken fire.

On the following day he repeated his musical performance, not accompanied by fire, for the benefit of a foundling hospital.

On April 13 Handel felt the whole Baroque horizon out far past London leaning over his bed after making for his house through the city's narrow alleyways, and he felt the street hurtling through the window from outside into his room, believing all the while that he was floating above his own body and experiencing his whole self, above and below that body, as a transparent reflector of sounds never heard before, now drifting through his chamber, opened out like the plains of the continent, toward which the horizon, along with Handel, leaned back again out of his room and far away, beyond the river, at a standstill, from which were clambering upward into the air sounds of which

Handel could for some time yet experience himself as the reflection and in comparison with which the onset of the echo from the first peals of the Easter bells, just now grown audible, must have struck him as the harsh clash of a shabbily rusted piece of scrap metal onto the surface of the sky, paved in a cobblestone pattern.

On April 13, exactly twenty-two years before, something similar had befallen him, though without the present abandon of so conclusive a definiteness. On that afternoon, his servant placed all the attention he could muster into the care he took in the performance of his duties, for the master, more furious than he had been for a long time, had burst thundering through the street door and gone foaming up the stairs, because in the theater the negligence of one or more members of a sloppily singing vocal ensemble specially hired by him had pushed him right up against the walls of his violent temper, so that he was able to check his outburst—just short of imminently threatening physical blows—only through the disappearance of his person, whose agitated pacing could still be heard above the ceiling.
These instances of carelessness during the course of preparations for the performance had passed beyond bearable limits; the performers cost him a fortune, that much was certain, but they were neither capable of nor concerned about making any of the fortune back.
He no longer considered them full of even enough feeling to sing in silence from the sheet music the stillness of a deserted room, a quiet that might have been drawn unseen on a yellowed piece of blank paper, and the emotion that rose up from his head had already broken through the ceiling to the attic such that the one need he now felt was to set thundering off the edge of the White Cliffs of Dover into the English Channel and foundering at the bottom of the sea every last one of the thousands of worn-out, illtuned, useless harpsichords that had ever been foisted on him in his life. Of course the frightened singers attempted to calm him down; they had sung the way he wanted them to, after all; what, he retorted, sung? no, he hadn't heard any such thing; people call that singing, do they? and what did that sound like? he, at any rate, was operating under entirely different ideas about the human voice. But of course it sounded, came the reply, exactly the way they had sung it as marked by him right there in the music;

and what did he mean, he hadn't heard any such thing, answered the singers, who wanted to prove their point by starting to sing again right away, but now Handel wanted to hear nothing more; stop! he shouted and covered his ears, stop singing at once; he couldn't listen to any more singing, and from now on there would simply be no more singing of anything.

Many of the neighbors had long thought of the house on Brook Street as a madhouse. At night, sleep-depriving chaconnes or sarabands would often resound from the surging harpsichord through the gateway, forgotten and left open, or there would sputter from the raised window a shrieking bellow when singing or a bellowing singing when shrieking, or else a singing shriek when bellowing in the calcified heroics of Italian opera conventions as they came from the throat of the German himself, now gone insane and pummeling himself menacingly about the head with his organs of song by producing tone so incorrectly.

Using soap bubbles that ballooned out and swelled up larger and larger, the servant had almost managed to shoo away the mocking racket of the ringdoves when one of his high-soaring spheres seemed to him to explode with such an exaggerated pop that he dashed up the stairs so he could be helpfully on the spot at once to repair a presumable household calamity. The room appeared empty, as if someone had just now left it, unoccupied the greasy sheen of the leather seat on the imposing general music director's chair behind the desk; he was preparing to leave when he saw the master motionless and rigid on the floor, his eyes opened wide, hollowed out in a fixed gaze, as if there were streaming through them not only the bygone hours of that day but, slowly, all the previous weeks and years as well, pouring out of his helplessly powerful body, flowing down through the stairwell, out by the gateway and onto the street, outward from the city as a more and more faintly audible groaning and wheezing ever farther off. The copyist had come bursting into the room, too, frightened, and in the shock of the fear they shared for the life of their master they laid his spasmodically twitching body onto the bed.

Then the copyist, leaving the servant with instructions to cool the collapsed victim's forehead with cold wet cloths, went storming out of the house. By happy coincidence there came driving past the equipage of a ducal patron, who recognized the man at once and stopped.

He cried loudly into the coach to please be so good as to come to the rescue by summoning the doctor, who immediately stopped studying the wondrous and splendid spectrum of his collected urine samples and, together with the copyist, drove through the streets in his little one-horse carriage to Handel; anxiously he rushed up the stairs and strode into the room, felt the pulse, bound up the arm limply drooping away from him, and pronounced loud and clear, as he invariably did at the beginning of every bedside visit, "Bleed the patient, don't you hear me, bleed the patient," a procedure which, by the way, represented practically his favorite activity as well as, in his opinion, a fundamental preventive measure always appropriate.

The servant had complied with his demand for a bowl, and the needle was already piercing the vein, out of which feverish blood came steaming into the vessel through an attached tube for a long time, until Handel finally sighed with relief.

Only through the helplessness he showed by shrugging his shoulders could the doctor answer the questioning glances of the copyist as to what was the matter. No slight fever, he then said, nor even severe fever, sorry to say, no angina, either, or, if anything, angina pectoris, in any case a temporary fainting spell, either through a sudden rush of blood away from the brain, or, on the other hand, perhaps, the possibility, albeit more remote in character, of a temporary occlusion to be accounted for by a sudden surfeit or oversupply to the head, an unfailingly predictable concomitant of the climacteric, incidentally; the sudden formation of large cavities in the curvatures of thought's pathways, and, as he could see, an unfortunate state, inasmuch as nothing was moving; for instance, the sudden forgetting by the one eye to execute properly the activity of blinking in the orderly fashion of prescribed regularity occasioning him to surmise, unfortunately, an apoplexy of some sort, a stroke, to be accounted for by excessive excitement in the course of the activity of taking nourishment too rich and far too ample, possibly also, by the way, if not almost surely, by excessive enjoyment of alcohol.

For four months he lived only in the left side of his body; without the other side, which he couldn't feel, it just drooped helplessly on the bed and lay heavy next to him. To his disgust, then, he had

become a constantly shackled and relentless prison guard to his
own self, one who kept him behind bars and padlocks the keys to
which had gone lost.

No word, no sound escaped his lips, sagging askew; his deadened
hand could commit no sign to paper. Only at times, when friends
would come to make music for him, did it seem as though the
tones and sounds were beginning to mirror themselves in his
eyes, as though the chains of melodies being executed before him
were being drawn inside his head through his pupils, while the
side of his body that could move attempted in vain to totter out
of bed and outside the house, as if he were trying to follow out of
the twilight of the sick room, through the window and into the
daylight, the soaring harmonies aflutter like a company of night
moths awakened in the room.

Mainly to provide him with some change in his helplessly stagnant condition, though hardly in the hope of much improvement—the thought of a cure would never have dawned on him—
the doctor recommended that the composer be taken to the
steam baths in the spa at Aix-la-Chapelle; perhaps the master's
afflictions would undergo a little greatly needed easing.

The journey now carrying the motionless man onward might well
have been prompting in him a short journey through the faded
storms of images in the memory of his constant journeys decades
before.

To Lübeck, for example. He had visited the most renowned master of the organ in the country, Dietrich Buxtehude, to apply for
the position of organist on what was then the largest organ in the
world, an appointment he would happily, even lovingly, have ac-
cepted and taken on had the taking on of the office not have been
linked to the altogether unavoidable obligation of also taking on
in the estate of matrimony the daughter of his old precedessor;
when he set eyes on her for the first and last time, however, close
enough so that the tragic breath of her pitiably innocent ugliness
grazed his face, he immediately announced his departure, somehow now urgently required.

Or, shortly thereafter, the journey to Italy, so decisive for him;
there the most distinguished and munificent patrons were soon
forcibly pressing into his hand keys to the entrance gates and

main doors of their summer residences, villas, and palaces, with entreaties for him to stay as long as possible and to grant them first priority in hearing his music.

Handel may have been the first musician who understood how to be addressed with requests, never orders. He did not sit, like Haydn even much later, at the servants' table, but was treated instead by the highest of dignitaries like a gentleman, one who was every bit as adept at dissecting an artichoke, a spider crab, a pheasant, a lobster, or a capon as he was at dissecting a chord or a scale. Almost everything that was vitally important to Handel had been invented in Italy. Probably even Italy itself. Hundreds of years earlier a certain Guido d'Arezzo had devised musical notation, only through which was it possible for Handel, among other attainments, to write down his music at all, and only through which the art music of the Western world, as it is called, was enabled to come into being. In Italy violins grew out of the ground almost along with the trees, built in under their bark, which subsequently created very few difficulties for those regarded still today as the most unsurpassed instrument makers ever in carving out of the wood instruments regarded still today as the most unsurpassed ever. Somewhat later, several "purists" or sticklers for first principles had attempted to reconstruct the ancient tragedies by precisely replicating their performance practice.

Out of what was perhaps a misunderstanding, characterized by many as embarrassing, there had then emerged the art called "opera." From which one might conclude that any especially inflexible resolve to adopt the most absolute purism and meticulous adherence to principle can lead either to an embarrassing misunderstanding or to epoch-making innovations that revolutionize whole centuries; or possibly, too, epoch-making innovations that revolutionize whole centuries might just as well represent an embarrassing misunderstanding. What had been brought about by that Italian misunderstanding called "opera," passed down along purist lines, was that people must have been offered a musical theater in which the performances would have been given mainly, if not exclusively, in the original Italian, even if they had no understanding of the Italian language. In those days there surely must have also been this or that composer who set piles of Italian libretti to music without understanding a single word of his own works. Similar to the Catholic Mass in Latin, perhaps, from which it would not be at all difficult, perhaps, for many to be tempted to characterize opera even today as a kind of ecclesiastical institution of higher secularity.

At that time, whoever came from Italy was granted immediate recognition and even world fame. That was why anyone who thought somewhat better of himself than average wanted to have been in Italy or even be Italian. Half of Europe thought better of itself, would much have preferred to rechristen itself "Italy," and accordingly imported Italian opera all over the continent. Handel to London, for instance. He had become well known in Venice with his *Agrippina*.

Through the course of the musical competitions inflicted on him over time he had encountered only on one occasion the sole musician ever judged to be his equal, Domenico Scarlatti, who at first surpassed him at the keyboard.

The sonatas by the Italian, cascading through the air with a bejeweled glistening of more colors than the eye could catch, had simply skittered away playfully from the daunting full-voiced quality of the German's passacaglias, which closed off whole spaces by filling them in entirely.

However, the audacity of his pianistic designs, his runs in thirds and his passage work in octaves, which often made his fingers look almost like flashes of light falling onto the keyboard, were later on simply ingested invisibly through the bellows and into the pipes of the organ, on which Handel surpassed him.

The most noteworthy of all his patrons had been Ottoboni, a cardinal, who had assembled along the walls of his bedchamber the almost uncountable number of his mistresses into a harmonious choir of oil paintings executed by the best artists in the country at that time; they were depicted as loosely clad figures of illustrious women saints, arranged according to the sequence of the Roman church calendar.

This cardinal, as he was called, had invited Handel to his Arcadian assemblages, as they were called, in the course of whose bucolic festivities the most distinguished notables in the country at that time donned perfumed shepherds' costumes to the accompaniment of a monotonous bleating from freshly bathed and painstakingly shampooed sheep, which they considered it incumbent on them not merely to herd but also forever to be dis-

posing to advantage; in the imitative architecture of their Augean
stables, cleaned every day by servants often tested to a Herculean
degree, and in the cantos of dilettantish epigones, whose pallid
verses, pale reflections of Virgil, hymned the unattainable beauty
of life in the country, they seemed to themselves to be remnants,
vestiges of bygone millenia, demigods in the ancient world's
scheme of nature, in which they expected that nymphs would
surface at any second from the purling streams, or fancied, as
they went scampering helplessly among the shrubbery, that they
had just escaped the wily magic of a hidden Circe, who had been
within a hair's breadth of transforming them into swine, as
which they most assuredly did not wish to be herded, much
though the bull who is the head god, having drawn near the im-
pregnably beautiful Europa and having perhaps already deliber-
ated about how he could hoist her onto his shoulders, will almost
surely never again be able to reach the point of swimming away
with her in the Tiber, let alone the sea, but will much more likely
prove instead to be an ox split open and turning on a spit over a
fire in some field.

Whatever had remained in Handel's awareness, whatever memory from those days lingering long afterward, might perhaps
have been sufficient to furnish him the idea much later for his
masque *Acis and Galatea*, that story of a shepherd who loves a
shepherdess and is loved by the shepherdess in return, though
there breaks in on them, because he is driven by burning desire
for the shepherdess, the frantic jealousy of Polyphemus, who, in
despair over the tranquil joy of the couple, one day drops a boul-
der onto the happy swain, positioned directly underneath him,
who, though dealt a mortal blow, yet persists, notwithstanding
being buried under a rock under a toppled mountain, in spinning
out his lamentations in song, which cause to surge up from the
rock a lamenting spring, whence there commences to flow
through the land, all the while cheerily extending its lamentation
as it courses along, a stream, one whose waves, however, are
made of nothing other than the garment, widening ever farther
out to the border of the region, of the shepherdess, who is continuing to lament in song the shepherd taken from her as she
makes her way along the water, following the waves which are
the train of her gown, until she herself goes cascading into either

the next river that crosses her path or into the sea, in the coursing of an estuary granting peaceful release.

While Handel was calling the singers over to the harpsichord so that they could continue rehearsing, the ballet master had requested permission to begin putting through their paces those of his pupils chosen for the performance, and in his ensuing gyrations he flounced about like a pest exterminator trying to shake a bug loose from the cloths he was incessantly flailing through the air while proceeding to bring on his choreographically trained pupils, exhorting them to mimic the way in which systematic movement is achieved without darting and dashing, as if one had just been sketched into a panel painting, calmly arranged with one's steady gaze turned toward the observers as they make their entrances from left and right at the exact same second, with utmost coordination; those from the right, in keeping with the incontrovertible rules of prevailing stage practise, representing something good and those from the left something evil (or else entering only at center stage, as if one were the very incarnation of the *deus ex machina*), exhorting them further to mimic the way in which, during a duel one could not refuse, one is supposed to be able to stab one's adversary, neatly and tidily, with a dagger or whatever other pointed object happens to be at hand, while engaged in standing fixed in any attitude whatever, or, less propitiously, in executing any movement in any time signature whatever.

What Handel mainly wanted to gain certainty about was whether the soprano, just a second before, when he had briefly turned his keenly scrutinizing glance away from her, had sung the high C on her own or whether her lover's castrato had once again trawled the note out of her throat for himself, because he was more skilled at hitting it than she, but then the snoring of Polyphemus, who had shut even the eye painted on his forehead (because of an exhaustion owing to daily rehearsals eight to ten hours long), seized him with a paroxysm of rage that forced him to leave the theater and that could well have brought on the stroke that would later divide his body at home.

But how much music was locked up inside him, seeking with ever greater urgency to make its way out, though seemingly trapped forever in a body incapable of movement, a closed cycle of har-

monies ever more densely impacted, enmeshed polyphonically to
an almost alarming extent by now, pervading him at moments as
a thing in frightening disarray, made up of all possible audible
tones resounding simultaneously, as if his head had chanced to
register the echo of explosions from the primordial sound made
by the splattering of a sun so distant and alien as to be conceivable by no one, as if the shadow of the noise made by its gradual
extinguishing through many millions of years of growing dusk
and twilight had wended its way behind his brow. His insistence
on finally opening himself out to everything once more and on
restoring order to his inner universe of sounds caused his lamentations to escalate ever more intensely and painfully, to be sure,
but at the same time it also caused him to grow ever stronger and
more determined in a way almost similar to the hot springs at the
spa, gushing out of the earth's interior, driven upward and outward by the heartbeat of volcanoes fallen dormant from the
steaming closed cycle of the planet.

From the start he had ignored the doctors, including their pusil-
lanimous caution about not spending more than three hours a
day sweating in the water for fear his body might otherwise grow
overtaxed by the mysterious power that emanated from the glowing core of the earth and bubbled up with the water driven
through the center of the planet. But his body could not have become any more overtaxed than it already was, and so he gave
himself up completely to the thermal baths, entrusting himself
blindly to their force, swathed himself in the steam of the geysers
as ardently as if he were making the interior of the planet embrace him in an effort to wash away and slip off the cage of his
body, almost as if he had dived down below the unexplored surface layer of the world so as to wrap it around him, in its entirety,
like a hot compress.

He would spend nine hours every day drifting through the water,
and it was as if his invisible prison were dissolving around him
little by little, breaking apart in the sulfurous clouds of steam. After only a week he was hauling himself without help through the
splendidly tiled halls of the grand baths, for movement was coming back into his wilted arm, and his lips, drooping and flabby,
began acquiring tension so they could form slowly regained
words and sentences, which in turn intensified his grateful astonishment to the point of amazed illumination, as if, along with all

the feelings and sensations to which he could once again give ut-
terance, much more had arisen that earlier had never immersed
itself in his memory, things he was able to sense but unable to
name.

On the day before his departure he strode through the great
spaces of the cathedral and up into the loft, to the organ already
opened for him. At first he began cautiously gliding a few fingers
of his left hand along the upper manual only, and then he
brought his right, fearfully at first, to join in on the lower manual, and when its fingers flawlessly obeyed his commands and
fulfilled his every requirement as well, he in gratitude pulled out
all the stops to set the whole interior of the stone ship surging
and flooding through the roof trusses, so that the slabs along the
sides began vibrating, while he imagined his body, now awakened to an agility he had never known before, as stretched
throughout the marble nave, full to bursting from the corridors
of the opened floodgates of harmony, and it almost seemed as if
this sacred edifice were moving, swaying altogether easily and
lightly, as if sail had been set outside on the tower over the roof
of this gigantic freighter built of brick for a journey now under
way, out across the flatlands of Flanders, to the coast, and across
the English Channel, transporting him back immediately into the
very midst of the island's capital.

He at once set to work harder than ever before so as to set down
in writing everything he had had to miss in the lost days of time
paralyzed, so as to liberate up onto the surface of systems on music paper all that had been dammed up inside him, now spread
out in an ordered musicality capable of sounding.

By way of mollifying his ducal sovereign—whom, in flat violation
of his contract, he had left in the lurch in Hannover for half an
eternity, and who, owing to favorable embroilments of kinship
on the one hand and to the childless state of the reigning female
English monarch on the other, was the designated future king of
the island—he ordained the flow of water music on the Thames,
that the river subordinate itself to his rhythms and not to any of
the gusts of wind springing up, that its waves beat in a dance to
the exact measure of his pipes and reeds against the walls of the
embankments and the sides of the ships gliding along it.

Soon enough, however, the bad times came back. First the death of the queen cancelled all public performances. Even afterwards, though, audiences stayed away, taken by surprise at the lack of money attendant on a war that had broken out over the Spanish succession or else glutted with the unrelenting seriousness marking the lofty demeanor–grown ever more incomprehensible to them in these weeks of crisis–of his rigid Italian-opera-style heroes in his *opere serie*, who came to be for these audiences either no longer refined enough or else too refined. The theater stayed empty, whereupon everybody deserted him, including, of course, Their Impudences the castrati, many of whom had been able to build themselves the most curious palaces from astronomical earnings (they bled him white) for what were often drastically inadequate performances of his arias, perhaps because they wanted to get back through him at what had been done to them as young boys by the unscrupulous pig butchers working for the fearsome conductor of the children's choir, whose thought was directed toward securing the continuance of the art of singing as he knew it and thus before whose mutilating power no beautiful voice approaching the onset of puberty could be safe.

What was more, his ability to conceive musical ideas, along with their power to enchant the senses, now seemed to desert him, for everything he defiantly attempted to compose, with ever more dogged determination, turned out under his hands to be merely pallid, limp growths, the shadows of sounds, until, the last remaining bit of his courage gone, he stopped writing.

Why had the hot springs not kept him for themselves, and why was he being subjected to so doubtful a release, he would ask himself whenever he went roaming, tired, through the wasteland of the overcrowded streets, which looked swept clean to him, appearing to him as if his feelings of inner despair, coming out of his own head, were settling in and weighing down the roofs, the streets, and the squares, as if his incapacity to create had wrapped itself around the houses as an immeasurable grieving.

And yet it was mainly a malicious grief, because the spiteful competition he had been facing for years was earning dazzling sums, and partly at his expense, at that, by robbing several of his works of their unrelenting seriousness and flinging them back out to a delirious public with satiric mockery, transformed into jokes that hit hard.

Yes, a significant part of his eclipse was thanks to that piece by John Gay, *The Beggar's Opera*, which audiences flocked to. As excitement over it mounted, interest in Handel seemed to wane, for now the public was faced with an evening of theater in which the aristocratic, hoity-toity arrogance of dukes on their uppers contracted marriage with the sly calculation of street prostitutes who couldn't get any lower and in the course of which several of his melodies, cleverly mangled into popular tunes, were tossed out from the stage with such admirably underhanded sincerity that even he was able to find some genuinely pleasing entertainment in them.

People were finally fed up, declared John Gay, fed up with flying gods, those airborne vagabonds, those winging vagrants of the sky, with stuffed and mounted lords treading the manicured ground as if on stilts, fed up as well with all those kind-hearted shepherds and shepherdesses dressed up in elegantly finished wolfskin coats; general interest had now shifted in favor of more traditional types–thieves, drifters, swindlers, beggars, procuresses, and receivers of stolen goods–and the language in which they conversed was no less choice, was altogether courtly, for that matter, even if it did keep itself hidden away in the murkiest corners of back courtyards.

Everything the public was looking for in the more celebrated operas could be found just as well in his own work, stated Gay, and his bare prison walls yielded nothing of the usual affect of devastating implacablity to grand choruses of captives in torment, so audiences could just continue to enjoy their soothing good cry.

Of course the esteemed public would not take well to Mr. Macheath's being executed practically as soon as he turns up.

But it was only natural that he should be, replied the hangman; if the play was to be structured with an apt poetic conclusion of the kind common with Maestro Handel, it would surely be more fitting to have him hang, because all the other hoydens and popinjays in the story, after all, had more than likely been either hanged or burned or banished, scattered to the four winds.

As anyone could see, lamented this would-be fugitive, this cream-puff captain in reply, it was only because he had broken out of jail that he was being sentenced to immediate execution.

That was why he was giving this good piece of advice to one and all: not to trust anybody any more, not your own people either, not even those who have confided in you most deeply, in which case you just might live a few months longer than you would otherwise.

And he indeed did not trust even his closest mistresses, the ones who could not bear the sight of a rope around his neck and would have preferred being hanged along with him rather than being left behind all alone; instead, he gave them no more than the well-meaning advice to get themselves shipped out to the West Indies, where they would surely be favored by the good fortune of landing at least one husband, if not two or three.

And then, after at least four of these women turned up with his illegitimate children in tow and wanted to be hanged with him, if possible, to take that journey with him, he began shuddering at the one thought of what would no doubt be quickly ensuing and rapidly mounting child-support payments in the celestial realm and the cosmic demands for alimony beyond this world of ours.

Through the damp, dingy tatters of darkness hanging down from the sky, Handel made his way that night back to his house, where all were sleeping. In his room he was overcome by melancholy memories of earlier times, when he would always bring home from his nighttime walks and at once get down on paper the new line of a melody tossed his way by a pert little wave leaping up out of the river's quiet monologue or by a few memorable chords from the drapery of the mild night wind spread out over the attics of the houses. But now, in these days and weeks, the very breathing of the awakened nights had begun denying itself to him, had judged him as no longer trustworthy enough to have committed to him the secret of deciphering its sounds. Or did the fault lie with him, his hearing, his intuitions, dulled by disillusionment over the calumnies of a fickle public made of all indifference?

His desk was empty, as always.

No, there was something there after all, something shimmering in the flicker of the candlelight, gently set in motion by the trembling and wavering of the flame such that it was visible even to his eyes, adrift as they were in slow helplessness. A packet, a letter from the poet who had cobbled *Saul* and *Israel in Egypt* into serviceably trimmed and patterned lines of verse for him.

Messiah was the title of this new text, one it had been suggested he might consider setting. Clearly the poet wanted to finish making a total fool of him, and besides, this was another one of these oratorios; how easily subject they were to every musical malady and every possible false intonation in their harmonic blend, and they hadn't gotten him much farther than where he was now.

On reading the first lines, however, Handel was enveloped by an inexplicably calming excitement, especially consoling to him in the state he was in just now; a resolute, intrepid feeling broadened out around him, as if everything had all of a sudden become entirely different. "Comfort ye, comfort ye, my people"—so he was meant to find comfort, he read on the page, and to be totally at peace, and from now on nothing would ever be able to plague or pester him again, for as of this moment in his life he was in such good hands that no one and nothing would be capable of getting at him.

It was as though a dry rain of sound were pattering down in a squall of harps upon the roof of his house, no, above all the roofs of the city and of all cities and villages, and it seemed to Handel that a fire had made its way into the room in which he kept on sitting, bent over his desk until he had completely filled page after page, a whole stack of music paper: but was it the fire of the thank offering—with its attendant flames to cool his head—that he was presenting by making it resound now, or was it the fire, sent posting to him ahead of time, in the middle of the night, of a day that would soon be breaking anew, setting ablaze the underbrush from the dried-out shrubs of a dawn that the east, torch held high, would send in spates from its far-off sunken place out past the edge of the ocean?

It was as though by personal effort he had fastened the ether itself to his desk, a sheet of paper spread out to clear view, correctly lined for notating music, and with hasty precision were inscribing the breaking of all seasons' squalls and storms all through the tidal movements of the nights.

In assembling or dismissing the choirs he sent sweeping through the measureless concert halls on every horizon, their voices, accompanied by the upsurging whispers of the woods, went swooping like flocks of birds through the opened cataracts of the sky en route to their settling of the atmosphere and, by the beating of their wings, tore whatever clouds they came across into little strips and tatters that hung far down into the fields of the lowlands, dispersed into the cheerful glow of trills, compounded of light and hail, drifting down from above.

Incomprehensibly natural-feeling lightning bolts of joyous emotion pierced Handel over and over, and happiness flooded through the composer like a fierce rain of pulverized ash rising up out of him and washing away the last remnants of the burnedout ruins' shadows in him, away into inaccessibly deep forgetting in the scrupulously clarified, serene lagoons of his remembrance, as if in company with his reawakening there had also surfaced realms, previously strange to him, inside a whole new world of feeling and knowing that he was able to sense but unable to name, or rather to name indeed, to transfer into sounds, and he was very close on the trail of every hidden mystery through the tones of the music he was just now composing, causing their solutions to rise up in audible sound, having shaped into clearly comprehensible, precisely distinct forms what hitherto could not have been fathomed, could not have been uttered, could not have been thought.

After three weeks the work was finished. Yet he still felt the lack of a roof over it, a night-sound audible roof overspanning the whole, reaching in its curvature into and through the atmosphere, a roof he wanted to draw with all the light-beam voices available, as if sung for the first time, over the mighty landscape of the work like a dome woven in its concord of resonance from all the flocks of swifts on the island, so that it would once and for all be as it should be.

On April 13, in Dublin, the work was heard for the first time. Since then, he had never again been thrown out of balance, even though he was still subject to the same vexations as earlier. Now, however, he was able to toss every effort over his shoulder with ease, the whole battery of jabs and sideswipes directed his way inflicted only wounds that did no injury, and he was able to pass through doors that had previously remained locked to him simply by walking past them.

The stairwells of the days and weeks and years lay spread out totally level before him on his still frequent journey through the many-colored church nave of the air in the radiance of the seasons, attended by the turmoil, transparent still, of the longing in the turbulent landscape images inside him, their emanation into his outward environment so strong, however, that their colors began to fade more and more, until his surroundings had come into such fine adjustment with the environs of his inner images that the images he saw spread out all around him had come to tally identically with the representations he was able to scrutinize in his deepest, inmost self.

Even when he had turned blind in his old age he did not stop seeing but saw instead through his measureless ear and then heard everything through the windows of his inmost eyes.

If with the passage of time he himself was in all probability no longer able to survey accurately the almost uncountable number of his works, so that he was perhaps beginning slowly, little by little, to take them back into some place of forgetfulness inside himself, as decades before they had come streaming out of him, the one that remained always present to him, that accompanied him everywhere, was *Messiah*. He loved the work, because he sensed himself to have been created, formed entirely anew, along with it. That was why he wanted to take leave of the public with it before resolving on a final retirement.

On April 6 they led the seriously ill seventy-four-year-old onto the podium at Covent Garden for the last time. His person had long since become an institution at whose appearance two candles, borne before him, were placed onto the harpsichord.

He sat there now as he had sat throughout his entire life up to this moment, remaining alone in the midst of a crowd he could not see; yet as the impenetrably dense choirs of returning clouds of migratory birds broke through the windows of the auditorium by way of the rising storm in the harpsichord and came soaring toward him, brushing against his eyelids–for they were now diffused in the cheering of the demonstrations, the vociferous ovations, thunderous by any reckoning, now being given him–his face, grown weary from the endless frequency of so many awakenings, glowed throughout the hall.

Frightened, they took him back to his house, where he lay down without ever getting up again.

And on April 13 Handel felt the horizon out far past the city go roaming through the alleyways and alight on his bed, while the street came hurtling through the window from outside and he believed he was floating above his own body, grown apprehensible as a transparent reflector of sounds never heard up to this time but now streaming back out of his chamber, which had grown as wide as one of the plains of the continent, while the horizon, along with Handel, leaned back again, beyond the edge of the city at the shore of the beginning ocean, quite far beyond the river, at a standstill, or, in this region beyond the city, simply stuck fast.

CATALOGUE D'OISEAUX

(For Olivier Messiaen)

1. Song of the Nightingale

Where can you be now, you winsome ones, hard-working chop-
cherry blackbirds
and other consumers of produce, and hard-working haunters
of fruit-entwined trelisses;
take wing now, you ravens, who follow the farmer
while plowing to pick the worms out of his furrow,
and where are you keeping yourselves, you gobblers of seed-
grain, who, cloaked
in the mantle of evening at twilight, gorge till your craws bulge,
you gaggle of barley thieves,
unbeloved watchers of olive groves,
bibbers before others get there, gourmets
of the vineyards and vintages;
and where are you, chirpers and screechers, wailers and callers,
and those who foretell, from out of the forests, the death dates of
those who will pass next
with such great precision and focus
that during a snow storm by night
there also come fluttering down
from the sky tiny announcements already printed;
where are you, hard-working mosquito destroyers, who help
keep the hoar frost of autumn's malarial freezes
confined to impassible swamplands;
kingfishers, ice birds, who sing with a squawking sound,
whistling high in the air your piercing icicle songs
out of hailstorms from far northern folklore
about faintly lit Arctic glaciers;
you hazel grouse, gold pheasants –
also you raptors, great sailing condors, bald eagles,
ospreys and chicken hawks, buzzards and kestrels;
when will I finally hear once more your chattery scolding,
you thrushes–has mockery left you? –

and finally hear your own call, brown-spotted snow owl, rare bird indeed,
whose call I've heard only from snow-foxes, living in fear of you?
They treat me by aping your cry, adding spine-chilling bellows of laughter.
Come finally gather around, you wailers, you gurglers and chirpers,
chatterers, cooers, and twitterers;
oh all you amaranths,
bristle-tails, sap-sucking woodpeckers,
wide-beaked bespectacled shrikes and blue-headed organists,
brood-parasite pouncers, undergrowth skulkers, earthen-cave potters,
yellow stub-tail blossom pickers, bullfinch-jays, cliff-dwelling nuthatches,
claw-snappers, windpipe-voiced craw-whistlers,
gorgers on mollusks,
pepper-eating trumpet terns,
red-tufted mockingbirds, ravine-scarlet crop-hooded tumblers,
you snowball marine hawks,
graybreasts, devourers of caterpillars, stilt-leggèd pointy-combed switchtails,
and you too, by all means, you church finches, great broad-billed cardinals,
rhinoceros-horn crested preeners, corncob-bassoon-sounding stutterers,
reed-cryers, shawm-throated squealers and bladder-of-bagpipe wing-flutterers,
why make me beg you so kindly today?

2. Chorus of Birds to the Human Race

Humans!
We were here long before you!
Take heed, oh humans, heed the beating of our wings!
As of today we are once more your rightful gods, just as in times gone by.
But that was so long ago you will have hardly any remembrance of it.

Our ancestor, the god Eros, escaped from a barren black egg laid
by the first primeval night–there was to be but one–out of longing for a second night, and with the goddess of infinity he begot
us, the first birds, firebirds,
even before there had come into existence time, which Kronos,
the god of time, held captured in the huge vessels of his lungs as
he copulated unceasingly with his wife, who unceasingly bore
him infants that their father Kronos would roast and eat like
suckling pigs.
These children, as children of an immortal themselves immortal,
would then, after they had been eaten and digested, be recopu-
lated anew by Father Kronos, over and over, back into the belly
of his wife, but for nought, only to be born anew, over and over,
but for nought, until one of them, Zeus, upon being born anew
yet once again after an unending series of birthhoods, all for
nought, secretly hid himself away and, with his mother's help,
grew up at a tremendous rate until he was big enough to slay his
father from behind.
But because Kronos as an immortal couldn't actually be slain, he
has ever since then–as part of a presumptive dying that is even
now still in process and that will continue to be in process until
the onset of eternity, far outlasting us–been exhaling not his life,
but our time, which has ever since then been seeping out of the
punctured vessels of his lungs.
Ever since then, by the beating of our wings, we birds have been
beating every second of time in its flight and showing the seasons
to you humans through markers and markings and the traces of
our flight across the sky.
　　As of today we are once more your rightful gods!
　　Open every cage within reach and set the birds
　　　free!
　　Only the song of the nightingale is keeping us reconciled,
　　　but no more than briefly.
　　Humans!
　　Heed at last!
　　Look upward, and heed more!
　　Yes; do not heed less!
　　From the night sky there escape
　　　echoes of songs

in the melt-water of northern light, glittering as it sprinkles
   downward:
starflake dust your last hope.

3. The Sap-Sucking Woodpecker's Litany of Sacrifice

Oh heed and hear us, God the Father of the Savior of our world,
which happened to you by accident, which no one wanted, no,
not you either, God our Father, though again and again you sent
a being into this unwanted world for us, your Son, our Savior, the
Redeemer, who will come again and again, who will have to come
to redeem every being that exists and has existed in this world,
oh Son of God, you who have redeemed the amoebas, because
God the Father sent you into the world as an amoeba to save the
amoebas, all the amoebas of this world, to take all the guilt of the
ameobas onto himself, as an amoeba, doing so for all amoebas,
despised and rejected and degraded as you were by all the other
amoebas while bearing the sins of all and sundry, of any and
every single amoeba that helped kill the frog, a creature with no
hair, and that after its cell division is again an amoeba plus an
amoeba child of parents who can no longer tell if they are the
parents or the children of their parents, since an amoeba doesn't
know, after all, if it's a papa amoeba, a mama amoeba, or a baby
amoeba, because how can a dividing cell tell the child and the
parents apart, and out of the waters from the sky have returned
to the Almighty who has forever and ever redeemed all the
amoebas in this world, though not by any means from this world,
for all amoebas have been saved ever since, redeemed because
they know that the amoeba God will call them to himself, into
amoeba paradise, where each one will sit at the right hand of the
amoeba Savior and probably at the left hand as well, and then life
crept out of the waters onto dry land and into the air, and
swarms of insects covered the land, along with all kinds of bugs
and roaches, and you redeemed all the bugs and the roaches, too,
and you redeemed the ants by becoming an ant and being willing
to take on yourself all the iniquities and transgressions of all ants
and in that way saving them from their sins, which you wound
onto the spindle of your slender ant's waist, and for that you
were bitten into little pieces by common female worker ants, who

then ate you, you the savior of the ants, redeemer of all ants, but you rose from the dead as a winged ant and flew up to God, the Lord, to God the Father, the Lord of all the ant-kings of the cosmos, all of whom you thereupon fertilized, as you continue now unto all eternity to copulate them so that they might lay eggs, thereby enabling and permitting those cosmic monster ants to enter our world soon for the purpose of being helpful to it when its own end has come, and also, God, Father, think always and ever of this or that bird among us, for as of now you have redeemed the wren, and you have redeemed the lark and redeemed the nightingale and the blue titmouse, the spotted woodpecker and the black woodpecker but not, for example, the sap-sucking woodpecker, which still awaits redemption through you, oh Son of God, that you might finally come into the world as a sap-sucking woodpecker and redeem all sap-sucking woodpeckers, might one day finally be willing to be a sap-sucking woodpecker and take the guilt of all sap-sucking woodpeckers onto yourself, or might deign finally to redeem one of those drab, stupid little sparrows, as one of which you have never yet come into the world, so be willing, finally, to become a stupid sparrow and take the guilt of all sparrows onto yourself, also not forgetting the sparrow-hawk warbling gnat and the sand-dwelling warbling gnat, which are birds, not insects, and not forgetting, either, the masked shrike, the harvest raven, the chaffinch, the lemon-yellow canary, the red crossbill, nor the blind crossbill, and you should not by any means forget the almost forgotten carmine-red bullfinch, though we do not wonder at your not yet having redeemed the wonderful ortolan, taking it instead as a comfort that in your great justice you mete out equally fair treatment to the most pathetic and the most beautiful and the most sublime in this world as well as the most worthy, God the Father and God the Son, for here, you see, is that shadowy fold-crevasse-ditch-gap in which a gathering storm, never yet actually having occurred, has grown stagnant and moldered away into the few weather-beaten remains of its own pitiful washout, one that you, Lord, did not prevent from discharging itself, but only, at any given time, the sins of this world instead! You have redeemed a few plants as well. You have redeemed the rose, redeemed the carnation, redeemed parsley, the tamarisk, and the peyote cactus, just as you also redeemed several mushrooms, the Venus fly trap, for example, as well as the intoxicating mushrooms of the Mexicans, which also grow in the Semmering mountain range and are given a taste in the underground darkness of some social circles in the capital cities of Europe or maybe just by people closer to home, say in places like Wiener Neustadt or Neunkirchen, where all I don't know, and in the same way you have already redeemed stinging nettles and climbing shrubs, and you will go on redeeming things and will continue to desire coming into the world as a thing, though of some very definite kind. You will redeem wardrobes, which also want to go to heaven, after all, so you will come into the world as a wardrobe and take all the sins of the wardrobes onto yourself, or, for instance, as a kitchen cupboard, or you will send your Son into the world as a backpack, for instance, to redeem all backpacks and free them from their sins, and the sins of sandals, too, and could you also please redeem the sugar bowls, too, and soon become a sugar bowl, oh Son of God, though the last time you came into the world it was as a case of hay fever and, as hay fever, took all the sins of all cases of hay fever onto yourself and, as one case of hay fever, were betrayed by all the other cases of hay fever, delivered into the hands of some ear, nose, and throat specialist, a doctor who just happened along but who to this very day has not let you rise from the dead, still holding you captive in the prison cell of a nutrient solution in his scientific laboratory instead, for you have remained up to the present time a case of hay fever and have still not risen from the dead, because you have not yet found a way to escape from the scientific laboratory and the abnormal nutrient solution in the research institute in which you are being held, not found a way to flee so that you might finally rise from the dead, all proper and correct, once again, but soon, when we come to help get you of there, dear Savior of the world, after we find out exactly where you are, of course, you must reward me by coming into the world next time as a crab louse, to take all the sins of the crab lice onto yourself, including what I'm about to say, which is—and you have to promise me now—that you will go to my girlfriend, who has rejected me and for which reason I will be unhappy forever, and lodge deep in the root of a hair in the mustache growing all around her second mouth, the one located between her legs, so that you might redeem not only all the crab lice in this world but also my girlfriend, whose second mouth you

should steer my way, oh Savior of the world, so that I might finally be happy. Then, in your work of liquidating this world,
which happened to you by accident and in which we are in every
way cleaning up after you and which no one wants, we will help
you, each and every creature contributing whatever possible as
well as it can, until you have personally brought about through
your Son the redemption, which for that matter you are still
bound to bring about, of every individual atom and quark and
neutrino and of all molecules. But because you are still a case of
hay fever, tucked away somewhere in your nutrient solution, we
might perhaps, as soon as possible, be sending the Holy Spirit in
the shape of a dove to help you, but it has to hatch first, and of
course nobody knows when it will hatch in the eaves of some
filthy attic. For until the very most minute of the very most minuscule, most diminutive, most petty, tiny minuteness of the tini-
est pettiness of the most minute, small, minuscule, petty, tiny
smallnesses which have to this day been hidden in unknown
places and are still being most carefully concealed as invisibly
small, minuscule, tiny, petty minutenesses in locations even yet
unknown are found, laid bare, and redeemed, all the rest of the
entire universe, this utterly idiotic and unnecessary cosmos will,
when all is said and done, have no choice but to sit around all
numb and dumb, its further redemption not allowed to proceed.

4. Chorus of Birds to the Human Race II

Humans! You are only half beings! Half beings cut off from your
own selves. Your ancestors were four-handed, four-legged human spheres in whose twinned, hermaphroditic bodies a man
and a woman were entwined in a ball and inseparably inter-
locked in such a complex fusion that they were unceasingly copu-
lating each other, all the while rolling all over the bumpy ground,
only stopping briefly sometimes to drop a few small baby
spheres, which, left to themselves, would start rolling over the
ground and scatter themselves evenly in the flatlands . . .
And so, strongly increasing and multiplying, you were one day all
assembled at the foot of Mount Olympus, of all places, where the
unbearable noise of your shrieks during copulation, by that point
multiplied many times by many thousands of times, disturbed

the immortal sleep of what was then the highest deity. Until there was no standing it any longer, so that they sent down to you from on high a team of divine assistant medical practitioners to perform surgically an operation that would one by one separate your parts into their two different constituents and then, having gathered together all of the mutually cut off other halves, to scatter them in every direction under heaven by blowing them to the four winds, another purpose being to have settled by your mutually cut off other halves those continents unknown to and unreachable by you at that time and accordingly still empty of human beings. Ever since then, and lasting right up to the present day, you humans, without even noticing it yourselves, have been searching for what is missing in you, with no chance of your ever finding it again, for even the direct descendants of those living generations of the other halves you are still missing, having meantime come to dwell on those other continents, which you have long since discovered, and, though being related to you by uncountably many removes of great-great and great-great-great kinship, have become so estranged from you that you fight them with great bitterness and destroy them as your most bitter enemies.

5. Closing Chorus

But now all shall be well.
No nail shall be afraid that a hammer might
smash in its head.
The heads of nails will not rust,
the thorns of roses will caress us.
Malice will no longer be dealt: friendly laughter
will thus be what spurs on the future of enmity.
Since people will no longer exterminate one another in
wars
they will destroy one another through bestowals of charity.
Future slandermongers will be able to injure us only
through
the deferential posturings of a respect moldered by dry
rot,

and rumors put about by even the most lowdown schem-
ers will cause
to sprout in the ears of their hearers nothing more than a
peace
tinged with longing for concord.
The thrashing stalks of stinging nettles will wrest release
from the prisons of gout,
and the withered fruit of the sticker bush will help heal
the rust wounds of stuck zippers.
Nothing but repeatedly verified proof of correct,
actual facts will make possible the buildup of new
errors necessary for the future.
For trees have come uprooted, have shot up into the air
like rockets, have fallen back down away from the light
out of highest heaven, headed straight for sawmills,
hurtling right into their circular saws
so that, sawing themselves into pieces on their own,
they could cobble together the tables and benches
on which we are sitting:
The heads of nails cannot rust,
and the thorns of roses will caress us.

Gentle Rage

or

The Ear Machinist

A Theater Sonata

CHARACTERS: LUDWIG VAN BEETHOVEN

                 ANTON SCHINDLER, HIS AMANUENSIS

                 FERDINAND WALDMÜLLER, A PAINTER

SETTING: ONE OF BEETHOVEN'S STUDIOS

Beethoven and Schindler will be sitting side by side, for the most part, so that Beethoven can at once read and immediately respond to everything Schindler communicates by writing it down in the notebooks of their conversations. The audience must imagine that Schindler, to shorten the entries in the notebooks whenever possible, will attempt to shout or at least to speak parts of longer communications into one of the hearing machines Beethoven is constantly wearing; the audience must imagine further that Schindler is certainly not writing down verbatim everything Beethoven has to say, whether a long communication or a monologue, but summarizing the content in key words, depending on how important the communication is. Even when the long communications and monologues are rendered as continuous utterances in what follows, one must imagine Schindler pausing fairly often as he writes, so that Beethoven will every so often be given a chance to grasp parts of longer communications while they are still in progress; with Beethoven's comprehension will usually come a grunt of approval or of ill temper.

Beethoven: My kingdom is in the air—
                I am what is—
                Shouldn't they be able to take some kind of
                clockwork mechanism and make a hearing ma-
                chine in which the motion of the air, always nec-
                essary to produce a sound anyway, could be ad-
                justed for my ear to hear, too?

                (*Sits down and pages through the* Intelligencer.)

                Lodgings for rent, a beautiful garden included;
                Landstraße 339—
                Housekeeper with culinary experience as well as
                household supervision—leave address in Wieden,
                at number 242, the house that had a fire—Life
                jacket invented by an individual from Verona—
                place the life jacket over the hips and buckle
                around the upper body, then inflate and screw
                shut —
                I could really use a few holders or cases for all my
                hearing machines—

Each man wants to belong to his light—

(*The hour strikes from the clock tower.*)

Two o'clock—so now we have the eclipse, starting
at 1:56 and ending at 4:39, according to the paper—at Schönstädst's optical shop, Rauhensteingasse 996, can be obtained functional sunglasses
or smoked glasses produced especially for the eclipse—

(*He stands up and goes over to the window to
observe the eclipse; while doing so he writes
what seem to be key words in his diary on a tall
desk.*)

The substance out of which the inhabitants of
different worlds, along with their fauna and flora,
are constituted, must be of a progressively lighter
and more delicate variety, the elasticity of their
fibers as well as the advantageous disposition of
their physical structure progressively more
sound the farther their distance from the sun—
The excellence of natures endowed with thought,
the speed of their conceptual power, the clarity
and vividness of the ideations they receive from
external stimuli, along with the capacity to combine them, plus the agility shown in their actual
execution—in short, the full range of their perfection—in the non-physical world as well as in all
materials, whether up somewhere in the planets
or elsewhere—all things must be subject to some
rule by which they perfect themselves with ever
greater exquisiteness in relation to the distance
of their dwelling from the sun—
Each man wants to belong to his light and to be
able to feel that he's a part of something somewhere—and I also want to teach light to learn to
hear—

(*He wipes his eyes with a cloth.*)

This discharge from my eyes keeps getting worse
all the time, even now, when I look right into the
blackened sun–I should start using linen cloths
instead of silk –
or maybe, on the other hand, only silk and no linen–Doctor Smetana is constantly making a
point of that, but then Schindler comes along and
claims that linen is better, so his doctor says–but
Smetana says silk, nothing but silk –
Perhaps the darkness that drips from my eyes
will soon place me in the position of no longer
having to decipher the stupid garbage people
write down in my notebooks; the darkness that
accumulates and thickens and bottles up in my
head until it comes pouring out of my face will
gush down onto the paper and wash away all the
writing. I would no longer see anything, and
there would be no writing to decipher, because
my eyes would erase the letters before I could
even read them–or, if I do want to read what's
there, I can quickly grab a silk cloth and wipe my
eyes, even though Schindler will say at once,
"Please use a linen cloth instead of that raspy
silk," or Smetana will say, "Nothing but silk, not
that rough linen"–none of it's worth wiping your
eyes about anyway.

My kingdom: the air.
My room: larger than any landscape.
Sometimes the whole Vienna Woods go sweeping
through the rooms of these lodgings –

Naturally I want to and have to belong to the
light that belongs to me–but the duskiness of the
twilight in this room grows ever more devious –
But then again, darkness is a kind of light–
granted, a kind you can barely see, but that's all
the better for hearing it so distinctly as the sha-
dow-echo sound-figure of a subdued remembrance of light –

More and more often I have to think back to my
childhood in Bonn—how I'd love to go back there
again, if only to climb up secretly into the rafters
of the house—even in those days the steep stair-
cases felt to me like mountain climbing—not as if
I were scaling the high range of heaven along the
outside of the mountain, though, with its dangerous ridges and burrs, but as if I were inside
the mountain, ascending to the peak through a
spiral-staircase cavern-labyrinth, not emerging
to the outside when I reach the top but as if remaining hidden inside, in the rafters of the ridge
and looking out into the countryside through a
window of rock in the mountain gables, through
a roof window in the mountain range –
By one of the roof windows in the attic of our
house there stood a dusty telescope that pre-
sented breathtaking views every time I looked
through it; I believe I was able to see out to the
Siebengebirge, that faroff, lovely line of mountains along the Rhine, and endlessly farther out
beyond even that. Somewhere past the hills far-
thest away, as they began to diffuse and vanish
along the horizon in the shimmer of the misty
sun, I could just about see fairly clearly, though it
was blurred, a house whose windows looked back
at me with disconcertingly familiar eyes. The
casement windows and the gleaming weather
vane signaled to me in the late afternoon sun
with their harsh flickering forced onto the glaring
light by the wind. It would burn into my eyes and
hurt as it blinded me. But that wasn't what would
subject me at times to a strangely happy fright:
out beyond the course of the river I discovered
on a hill set almost over the horizon not only this
house, which appeared to me an exact mirage
replica of our house in Bonn, situated over there
in that outlying region, but more specifically I
discerned in a roof window in the distant gables
the very same telescope looking back at and pre-

cisely trained on me. Of course the question that
came to mind at once was who–who, aided by
the directed, focused solar reflection signals of
his telescope's eye, was sending me from over
there the coded light flashes of his messages; on
my end, I attempted to answer immediately by
the same means, although I didn't know what
there was to answer or how I should go about it–
but I seemed to meet with success in transmit-
ting something or another back across the almost
transparent hills in the middle distance, even
when I didn't quite know what or how (somehow
they understood me), but one day I somehow no
longer knew whether I should feel more som-
berly jovial, amiably frightened or else joyfully
downheartedly amazedly soothed at peak stimu-
lation, because what I recognized in a hazily distinct way standing behind the faroff telescope in
that unreachable roof window was someone not
only similar to me, but, as I saw with a misty
kind of acute clarity, my very self looking from
over there directly at me in Bonn, in my attic
window, behind which I would be standing like a
stranger and looking through the telescope, but
deep within, facing my own self and vice versa.
In either place it seemed to me that I was equally
and unreachably remote from myself, though
constantly tossed back and forth, moment by
moment, hither and thither, ever and anon, from
myself to myself, a living mirror image in the air
or an apprentice of light awakening to life –

That might just possibly be a solution for me: not
hearing in and through air any more, catching
the vibrations and oscillations of the tones
through it, which has become impossible anyway
with my hearing well-nigh totally vanished, but
instead listening more intently to the light from
now on so that I can take in, via my face, the
movements of the sound floating on the waves of
light, the songs of the air borne to me by light

beams and perceived when I capture them with
my glance –
For example, having the sounds of a quartet conveyed to my eyes, instead of to my ears, by the
lighting in a salon or an auditorium, so that I
would soon learn how to take in, with utmost accuracy of these altered perceptual faculties, the
chords adrift in the room and wafting their sono-
rous way toward my head amidst much flickering
of candles –
To try something like that with all my might, anyway –
Of course I would have to put up with stirring
abroad only on cloudy days or going out only at
twilight and staying inside my lodgings at other
times, exposing myself as little as possible to full
sunlight; otherwise the blinding sounds of its
constant light-beam singing at highest pitch
would cause my glances to grow deaf as well, because the piercing lamenations I hear to my own
peril in the sunbeam dissonances of the midday-
light orchestra would make the eardrums of my
eyes burst –

It hardly bears thinking about, incidentally, if
one day some cosmic change in our present circumstances were to cause everybody in this
world to apprehend the sun not only by its light
and to feel just its warmth, but also to hear it and
thenceforth, assuming such a hypothetical case,
to have to contend with ensuing new phenomena
likely to be on the unpleasant side; let's say as a
result of some cosmic curiosity like an unimaginably long and thick air resonance hose that, to
the total astonishment of the world, would be
found to have traveled across or through space
from the sun and attached itself like a monstrous
umbilical cord to our earth: an unbearable noise
from the sun, an unimaginably fierce pounding
and atmosphere-shattering of sunlight-
demolition weather booming, sunbeam shrieks

that explode upwards in air, in the crashes of
light persistently gaining strength toward a rain-
bow-rumbling midday that, with its thunderously
reiterated horizon crashes and the firmament
eruptions, so piercingly pulsating through the
entire space, of its commencing, ear-splitting, af-
ternoon-illumination down-hurtling cataracts,
down from the sky and bursting on the ground,
smashing to smithereens the heads of all passers-
by –
Only sometimes comes a let-up in pace or a saving grace caused by a few yearned-for cloudy
days, moderate and muffled to shadows of
sounds; or else, audible still, but solely in the remaining peaceable nights, a faint, black, altogether menacing echo of rolling as if the sounds
of a faraway battle from the other side of the planet were surging from there, where it is day, to
the night that has advanced on us, only for the
unceasing storm of summer sunlight to resume
all the louder at the break of dawn on the eastern
horizon –

The hearing machine could be built such that
stars at the opening make the entrance of the
sound easier, disseminating the sound around
the whole ear and allowing one in that way to
hear at every opening –

(*Turns away from the window.*)

It's cold here. Probably this cool sunset, pushed
by the sky into the room through the closed window. Or maybe it's finally time to demolish this
old stove and install a new one. That would make
for a good dispute with Schindler; he's a good
deal more suited for a talk about heating stoves
than for exchanges about music, during which he
is constantly jumping in much too impulsively.
But never let your disdain for anyone show on
the outside–you never know what you might

need the person for.

Enter Schindler. After he tries to speak his first sentence directly into Beethoven's ear-trumpet without being understood, both men go over to the table and take seats side by side. The following dialogue proceeds with the help of the notebook, though Schindler will also intermittently attempt, rather ineffectively, to make use of sign language.

Schindler: I checked through the score of the quartet and ending up finding the mistake after all. It is an extraordinary honor for me to be able to lend you a hand from time to time, whether in practical or muscial concerns, during the course of which activity I shall give myself great pains to be most assiduous in taking matters off your shoulders.
On Sundays and holidays I am to be found at home, sitting diligently over the sonatas. The next time I am able to come I shall play several of them for you by way of testing all the things I wanted to keep in mind about my good intention of noting since the last time. I'm still struggling with the notes, however.
That discharge from your eyes has yet again grown worse, I note; you should invariably use a linen cloth to wipe your eyes, never silk.

Beethoven: It's the eclipse that's making my eyes run so much.

Schindler: (*pointing to a place in the open* Intelligencer)

You should have obtained functional sunglasses or smoked glasses produced especially for the eclipse at Schönstädst's optical shop on Rauhensteingasse –
Or blacken a piece of glass with soot and hold it in front of your eyes to protect them from injury when looking directly into the almost black sun.
I suggest going to my lodgings. It's warmer there, and we will be less disturbed as well; your ser-

vants are forever skulking around behind doors, and surely they must often disturb you.

Beethoven: No. We'll stay here. My servants do not disturb me. I never hear them, which is very pleasant— one of the incidental advantages my hearing impairment confers on me, by the way—and less and less often do I ever see anything of them, either; not that the whole pack of thieves is hiding because they're scared or afraid of me, but more because through their idleness and laziness they've entangled themselves behind my back in all kinds of lying, cheating frauds and intrigues, often proceeding with such diabolically nasty refinement, thanks to their extremely open-hearted audacity, that you wouldn't consider the highly intricate nature of their simple impudence even possible. They go through a charade of entering in my expense book eighteen gulden as the monthly bill for a single breakfast roll every morning. Not long ago I grabbed from the shelves all the books I could get my hands on and hurled them at the head of one of the maids; apparently some of the content must have whacked its way into her brain, because she's making ever so slightly more intelligent faces than she used to, although she still can't get out of the habit of allowing her features to take on the most idiotic look possible when she's carrying wood up from the cellar. I should kick the whole gang of them out. But where were we? Oh yes, we're staying here, not going to your quarters.

Schindler: Dear master, there come at times moments in which a man feels free to complain about his fate. I had no choice but to pursue a career in the law. I would have preferred a career in diplomacy, except that such a thing is not possible without family financial resources.
If my dear patron and mentor Count Herberstein had only remained alive just a short while longer,

I would surely have become a nimble diplomat–
without doubt a second Talleyrand. I would immediately have put a stop to the Neapolitan revolution by a diplomatic bleeding, and that would
have taken care of that. But with all the kinds of
horses' asses who at present are exercising their
stunningly exasperated (*stuttering*) proficiency-
deficiency throughout Europe, there's nothing to
be done.

But I do have an advantage, after all, in that I can
now occupy myself ever more intensively with
music, which has turned from an essential incidental to an incidental essential–from my intensive study of theory to my practise on the mecha-
nisms of many musical instruments. But you
know all about my activities anyway.

Beethoven: So then instead of a frustrated diplomat you've
decided to take a stab at working your way up to
the status of diplomatic musician, and, in your
quest to arrange various matters as you'd like
them, you're no doubt working from the most
upright of intentions.

Schindler: Well, I am over twenty years old, and my brain
matter still isn't working full tilt. But maybe
something will suddenly go bang inside my head,
and everybody in the room will take fright, because they've never been in the presence of a
head that made such a loud bang, and quick as
lightning too, you know. Then I would be in-
spired.

All right, but if I can't induce you to come to me,
then you might have just a little time now–I can't
make anything of the largo movement of the D-
major sonata–time to go through one certain passage with me. Would you mind? Just once, then
I'll retain it permanently.

Beethoven: I have a different sonata in mind, a brand new
one, one I don't think you'll ever be able to get

under your fingers, or if you did, your fingers
would go totally mad, completely insane, and for
the rest of your life you'd have to lock your hands
away in a madhouse, which you'd then always
have to carry in front of you. So as I've just said, I
have a whole new kind of sonata in my head, so
that it just wouldn't work for me to give you any
instruction, no matter how brief.

*(Beethoven goes over to the piano and puts into
his mouth a thin stick that reaches from his lips
deep into the open piano.)*

Schindler: *(very loud, almost shouting at Beethoven before
the composer starts playing)*

Tell me, are you really able to hear your work better, or even to hear anything at all, when you
draw for help on that stick you place between
your teeth and then dangle into the sound bed?

*But Beethoven has not heard the question, so he begins playing
the opening of the Hammerklavier sonata, op. 106, but wildly
and badly, because he hits so many wrong notes.*

Schindler: I'm sorry to say I have no idea what you've got in
mind with those violent chords, and you're play-
ing far too loud, because without your hearing
you have no control over any instrument. Or
could all this elaborate racket be a component of
the sudden new development in your music? Of
course I can also sense a gentle frenzy, almost
with a highly disciplined kind of disorder, in a
kind of affectionately thundering power, as if you
were trying to open people's ears fully, to convey
some sense of your deafness to your listeners.
Even so, I can't make heads or tails of it; it really
mustn't go on this way.

Beethoven: *(has not altogether stopped playing, but is allowing his hands to improvise, almost as if on*

their own and as an afterthought while he is
talking, several of the main harmonies of the
first movement, the exposition of which he plays
to its first conclusion)

Time to stop your nonsensical claptrap! Oh, I
can't hear what you're saying, of course, but I'm
certainly in a position to read it clearly from your
facial reactions! You sense only too well that I'm
using those chords to deliver unmistakably a few
swift kicks to certain very particular individuals,
and I sense you're not at all comfortable with
that.
What I actually have been wanting to talk to you
about from the minute you got here today,
though, is that for the longest time I've been having trouble with my stove now, and I believe that
as a frustrated diplomat you're somewhat more
familiar with stoves than I am, for I understand
only how to fire up people's heads through their
ears, as it were, in saying which one could draw
an apt comparison between people's ears and
stove doors.
But no, my stove here is useless. I've been wanting to tell you that for a long time and ask if you
couldn't come to my aid by offering pertinent advice.

Schindler: We talked about this in detail not long ago. The
master stove and oven fitter will have to come in
the near future with his apprentice workers to in-
spect the problem and set it right. You'll have to
make a special point of calling his attention to the
location of the stove. Because of where it stands
now, all the heat is going into the walls; the room
isn't getting any warmth. It seems to me that the
first job would be to move the oven farther away
from the wall and to break away more of the wall
from above the stove; otherwise it can't heat the
room, but only the tile wall surrounding it.

Beethoven:	I understand. That would be the same as if a piano were backed against a wall, so that when it's played you hear very little in the room itself, if anything, because all the sounds being played are sucked up by the wall, swallowed by the masonry. That wouldn't make a bit of difference to me, incidentally, because with my impairment I wouldn't be able to hear a thing in the room anyway, and I would actually be much happier if the walls were to swallow up every tone, chord, harmony, and melody before they ever reach me and my ear, which they can't enter at any rate; at least I would know for certain that my ears aren't missing anything, because the sounds would all disappear with well-nigh effortless ease into the ears of the walls just before having to confront, with utmost strain, the task of at last finding shelter in one of my ears, without of course achieving the slightest success and thus having to wither away in some room somewhere or to freeze to death or evaporate somewhere outside. Many thanks for your outstanding considerateness, dear Schindler, and I hope I may expect to see you here again soon. I will, won't I?
Schindler:	I shall at once allow myself to construe it as the most pleasant of all my welcome duties.
Beethoven:	(*alone, standing at the window, which is now open*)
	The wildly surging silence of the woods! The wind, rising now when the weather is good, without getting caught right away in the tangle of sunbeams ripped apart by a shower of spring hail–that wind can no longer keep me in Vienna, because it's my enemy! To develop hearing machines to their full capability–finally–so that I could then finally travel, get away from here; maybe I could really go to England at last!

But now a *Föhn*, that dreary, gray, heavy wind, is
once again blowing into my head through my
ears, and then it turns rotten whenever it loses its
way hopelessly in the labyrinths of my brain's
convolutions, stuck somewhere in some forgotten
corner at the back of my head, where it falls asleep, completely drained and exhausted. Or, almost entirely powerless, it sneaks its way behind
the back of my face and gets squashed or completely ground to dust and sifts down my back into the whole rest of my body, which then feels ill
at ease –

(*sitting back down, partly reading from the* Intelligencer, *partly making notes*)

Hearing machines made so well that the sound
enters not only from the side, but straight on as
well–and they should also investigate what shape
would be best: round, oval, elliptical, cone-
shaped, cylindrical, or pear-shaped; it would
make no difference to me –
Perhaps I should purchase an electrovibrational
machine, the effect of which is directed mainly to
blocking any intensification of electrical impulses
generated by a rheumatic whistling in the ears,
no matter how persistent, and which can be almost without exception successfully brought to
bear, and with outstanding results, at that, in all
cases of advanced hearing loss or even total deafness; can be obtained at the Sulfuric Fumigation
Institute on the Hohe Warte –
Mödling: house for sale in Soos near Baden, 1,553
cords of black pine, the predominant type of
wood – Don't forget boot polish, hand soap, blot-
ting paper –
The latest postal travel book issued under the official sanction of the Royal and Imperial Main
Court Postal Service Department, bound in pig-
skin or in paper, available at Kautfuss and Arm-
bruster's, Singer Strasse 957 –

Schindler:	*(comes into the room and sits next to Beethoven at the table)*

It's frequently very fitting and convenient for one person to be available to another, since people are prone to look to their neighbor for whatever they're lacking. That's the basis on which it will be necessary for you to make comprehesive written records of your ideas on the spot, and then I will immediately put them in some kind of order.

Beethoven: Would you know where I might be able to purchase a commode at the most reasonable price? And then I also urgently need a chest for all the stupid clutter I now have temporarily hanging on wooden hooks; or maybe I could use it to store my clothes and linen.

Schindler: Perhaps you could try putting an object of the same dimensions in the place where you mean for it to stand. What is new and original gives birth to itself, you recently said, however, without any thought being given to the matter.
Doesn't taking action mean composing in your case?
It's an unusual course of action, after all.

Beethoven: *(jotting down key words now and again)*

Or an illuminated oil-fueled night-light clock. Or maybe a sofa. What about a chandelier, or instead, and even better, a few night lanterns similar to the gaslit lamp posts on the streets?

Schindler: I shall make every effort to be on hand for you in these matters.

Beethoven: Have you by chance paged through Ernst Florens Friedrich's new textbooks *Acoustics* and *New Approaches to a Phenomenology of Acoustics*?

Schindler: No, but at the Chamber of Natural Curiosities on
                  Josefs Platz I found some information about a
                  new kind of sound amplification machine devel-
                  oped by a certain Doctor Bremser.

                  (*taking out a slip of paper*)

                  I've also been hearing about a Doctor Pohl who
                  for many years has been studying and writing
                  about nothing but the anatomy of the ear and its
                  diseases. He's also said to be very musical. I quote
                  him: "Diseases of hearing, or reliable methods of
                  alleviating and gradually curing hardness of hear-
                  ing, buzzing in the ears, and even total deafness,
                  together with instructions and methods for main-
                  taining the ears and the faculty of hearing in good
                  condition, correcting the defects of same or fore-
                  stalling them in the first place and remedying
                  troublesome compulsions of the ear, as they are
                  known." End quote.

Beethoven: That last term probably refers to the best way of
                  learning how to force oneself to forgo the use of
                  one's ears entirely, not to have to be dependent
                  on them or to be obliged to use them at all: not
                  compulsion of the ears, but forfeiture of them.
                  Yes, indeed, voluntary forfeiture of the ears,
                  committing this excess in an ascetic sort of way–
                  that's the indispensable exercise for heart-
                  strengthening unreliability and undisciplined
                  loyalty to principle.
                  Can you still remember, by the way, those two
                  delightful singers from Leipzig who requested to
                  sing passages from *Fidelio* for me and who then,
                  after my joyful agreement, became terribly em-
                  barrassed all of a sudden and couldn't produce a
                  single tone, hindered by the fear of possibly not
                  doing it right in front of me, the composer, whe-
                  reupon you were able to explain prudently to
                  them that I am hard of hearing, or for that matter

totally deaf and I could then call out to the singers: "You know, I didn't want to *hear* you sing; I
only wished instead to *see* you singing."

Schindler: Yes, and so what we see once again is that in
Germany singers are there for the composer,
whereas in Italy the composer is there for the
singers.
Rossini was recently in town again, by the way.
He was very eager to call on you, just as he was
during his last visit, but he couldn't quite manage
it after all. Still, he wanted to convey through me
his very warmest regards; now he's gone again.
Lately, I happened to make the acquaintance of
some count whom neither you nor I had ever met
but who seems to know all about you. This count
said he knows a way of restoring your hearing,
and it was his express wish that it should be
communicated to you and conveyed through me
with a certain amount of urgency. He told me
about an experience he'd had with his wife, who
lost her hearing but then regained it by a simple
means. He urged me not just to write it down for
you but also to have you try it out immediately
under my supervision.
You take fresh horseradish when it's just been
pulled out of the ground, grate it onto two scraps
of cotton, wrapping them up quickly and then
stuffing them into both ears as deep as they will
go. This has to be repeated as often as possible,
but always–every time–with horseradish that's
just been pulled from the ground, grated, and
rolled up as fast as possible in cotton scraps, then
stuffed into the ears as deep as they will go –

Beethoven: As you say, as often as possible–days, perhaps–
weeks–years–decades, perhaps–even centuries,
maybe through many lifetimes –

Schindler: Exactly so! You're right, because the count personally witnessed, as he stated himself, that his

wife supposedly regained her hearing through this simple means in a matter of four–or was it forty–weeks–or was it years. I can't remember now. Anyway, the treatment the count described to me had just been successfully completed.

Beethoven: And of course the only way he could ease his fear that his wife's newly restored hearing might be for the short term only was by the process of starting over and over from the beginning, never ceasing until her hearing is recovered once and for all, after she's dead, that is, in her next life–

Schindler: You haven't made any attempt for a long time now to play your upright piano, your console. I wonder why not. Stein believes you couldn't have anything better.

The notebook with them, they go over to the upright piano, and Schindler takes out a sketch.

Schindler: His thought is to seal up the front for you and thus make it completely soundproof. Then he would install two trumpets that could be pressed against your ears, held secure with a strap, and be fastened airtight with rubber suction cups. Tomorrow Stein will conduct some tests, either in his own home or here, with you. The problem is that the frame around the cabinet mustn't be mounted too high, because you can't very well play the piano standing up, after all.
Also, he has a brand new idea for your concert grand. He's hoping it will do you some good:
He wants to secure a dome-shaped cover that stretches from the front to all the way in the back so that no sound can escape from the top or the side.

(To help Beethoven visualize this fixture, Schindler takes him over to the grand piano, holding the notebook.)

Schindler: This arch or dome will supposedly be fashioned
               from very thin resonating wood, and it has the
               enormous advantage of leaving the keyboard free
               without letting any sound emerge. All the sound
               stays inside the piano; not a single tone can be-
               come audible by taking flight outward, and only
               your head, you understand, or something along
               those lines, as was explained to me–anyway, your
               head, inserted in some way, screwed in, built
               somehow right into the cabinetry of the instru-
               ment and sealed off, bolted, if I understand cor-
               rectly–at any rate, only your head is thus fully ex-
               posed to the whole range of sound from the pi-
               ano, and because virtually not one single note can
               escape your ears, nothing would be lost to your
               hearing, whatever it might be able to apprehend
               or rather not apprehend, for on the outside of the
               piano almost total silence would prevail, even
               should execution upon the instrument be very
               forceful. Only on the inside, in the resonance
               chamber, is the entire gamut of sound reserved
               solely and most exclusively for your head, em-
               bedded and affixed therein.

Beethoven: I could really wish that such an instrument might
               be supplied to most of the pianists appearing
               these days, for then we would never have to hear
               another note of their featureless playing, which
               would represent an extraordinary boon for the
               majority of our concert undertakings. The intro-
               duction of pianos like that, silent to audiences,
               would be a highly praiseworthy arrangement,
               much to be recommended to many concert man-
               agers, and an enrichment of our musical lives.

Schindler: But if the man is going to do that for you–and if
               he does, the first change is that those odd sticks
               you always clench between your teeth and then
               dangle into the resonating sound bed will most
               likely come to be altogether unnecessary–if he
               does, I say, you'll have to have your piano sent to

him. I could make all the arrangements for you, if
you'd like. I'm always here for you. What he
would then do first is to prepare for you here at
home a sample-shaped pre-production model
(*stuttering*), or I mean a sample pre-shaped
modeled production, or rather a pre-sample
model-shaped production sample. I trust I have
conveyed all of this to you as clearly as possible.
Do you think perhaps I should instruct the servant girl to go into the garden and pull up some
fresh horseradish, which we would then grate
onto two scraps of cotton to be rolled up and
stuffed into your ears as deep as they will go?
At least it can't do any harm, and Doctor Smetana
thinks so too.

*With an annoyed motion of his hand, Beethoven sweeps Schind-
ler out of the room.*

*(Optional: the computerized piano plays the middle section of
the scherzo from the "Hammerklavier" Sonata, either to the end
or to the rapid run.)*

Beethoven: (*alone*) Fortunately I haven't blundered into one
                    of those sound-space cages any time lately, but
                    up until recently I used to become temporarily
                    entrapped in them every so often –
                    I suspect that's the reason I was barely able, at
                    least not until a short time ago, to compose any-
                    thing that would cohere: I was incapable of actu-
                    ally allowing one note to follow the one before it,
                    because there was something compelling me to
                    keep on waiting; between the two notes there
                    would finally have to occur a silence hitherto un-
                    known, of an entirely new kind, musically speak-
                    ing, simply never yet heard by any accessible ear,
                    whenever, wherever, or however –
                    In order to notate musical silences resounding
                    with such intensity one would have to devise and
                    apply something altogether different from the
                    conventional indications for rests–it's the same

as when a person gets stuck, as often happens, in
the middle of a sentence or a thought and doesn't
articulate the word that's about to come, not even
in thought, because one is hoping between two
words or shreds of thoughts for some recognition
illuminated in muteness –
a kind of silence in a foreign language, to be acquired with great drudgery and by the help of
which so much could be so clearly concealed that
it would finally yield to a more accurate understanding than it has up to now.

*The painter Ferdinand Waldmüller enters the room, sets up his
easel and canvas, and begins painting Beethoven, who is sitting
for him.*

Waldmüller: What's it like when you speak? Do you hear your
                own self when you say something?

*(Notices that Beethoven does not hear him, so he gets up from
his easel, goes to the notebook, and writes the question, which
Beethoven then reads, while Waldmüller returns to the easel.)*

Beethoven: Sometimes my voice will grow audible to me in-
                side my head, because it does not have to depend
                on my hearing and can find its way into my brain
                independently of my eardrums or other organs of
                hearing. Sometimes, I say, but not always, if what
                you mean is that I understand nothing coming
                from the world around me but myself and myself
                only; it makes no difference whether I'm talking
                to myself or with others. It can also happen, too,
                that whatever I'm saying to myself or other peo-
                ple is immediately tossed right back outside my
                head, before I can hear it, by some kind of echo-
                ing wall inside my skull. I think it may also be the
                case that words my voice may have just framed–
                because they are hurled outward from my brain
                so fast and with such force–are bound to be
                heard by my listeners as being at least twice as
                loud once they're outside me as they were when I

spoke them to begin with. Of course I can't verify
that. How would I be able to ask somebody,
"Doesn't what you just heard me say sound to
you at least twice as loud as I said it a moment
ago, inasmuch as every sound is flung right out of
my head well before I can discern that it's audible, and anything I say races off and away into
the air in such a lightning-quick frenzy that it
seems to want to escape from me, as though my
own thoughts were afflicted with panic-stricken
fear of my own self"? Could I ask that? But then
something entirely different can come about as
well, the exact opposite, in fact. Sometimes I've
hardly uttered what I have to say than, instead of
penetrating outward, it is flung back into my
head by those inner echoing walls, but reversed
now, so that I'm certain that not a single one of
the words I've just spoken could possibly have
been heard, by contrast with which everything
sounds so loud inside my skull that I can't comprehend a single one of my own words, because
what's become snarled behind my brow is nothing but an unintelligible jabber of buzzing and
ringing. And how can I determine whether anything I'm voicing makes its way outward and is
heard unless I ask, "Are you aware that I was just
now trying to say something definite to you, and
do you think the reason I might possibly have
failed is because my words are pulled backward
out of the space between you and me at the last
second, sad to say, back past my lips and into my
mouth, intercepted, trapped, falling back somewhere inside my head before they reach your
ear"? Could I ask that? For some time now, however, I've often been unable to hear anything at
all that I say to myself or others. I could con-
ceivably be spouting the worst kind of feeble-
minded gibberish and not be able to hear or understand a peep of what I'm saying. Then I truly
no longer comprehend myself, though admittedly
with a sharp-sighted clarity of the humdrum sort

or with a clear-sighted perceptual sharpness of
the murky sort, both states helpful to me in having at my disposal a harebrained body of knowledge developed to its peak point and in being an
almost dimwittedly omniscient dolt.

Waldmüller: And how do things stand with you right now?

*(Notices again that Beethoven has not heard, so
he writes out the question in the notebook.)*

Beethoven: I'm not really quite sure. But I can ask you this:
Does what I'm saying sound at least twice as loud
as I uttered it just a moment ago? Or is it possible that nothing of what I'm saying can even be
heard?

*Waldmüller signals Beethoven by a hand motion that every-
thing has been spoken and heard very clearly.*

*Schindler enters, stands next to Waldmüller and watches him
painting.*

Schindler: *(to Waldmüller)* Haven't you heard? The day before yesterday a salami maker stabbed a painter
with his butcher knife. Yesterday they rounded up
all the salami makers and threw them in jail to
find out which one did it. But nobody gave the
culprit away. So they couldn't find out anything
definite and had to release them all. Hadn't you
heard anything about it?

Waldmüller: *(shaking his head)* No, but perhaps the aforesaid
artist, the painter, that is, daubed an especially
choice salami produced by the aforesaid butcher
onto one of his egregiously botched still lifes in a
manner injurious to said butcher's reputation
and consequently to his business, which then
could very well have induced in the distraught
salami maker the headlong compulsion to proceed to his rather immoderate action.

Beethoven:	(*who can't hear anything, to Schindler*) Schindler, my friend, please write down for me, at least in summary form, what Waldmüller is saying to you. He can't be writing and painting me at the same time, you understand.
Schindler:	(*to Beethoven, next to whom he has taken a seat, writing and bellowing into Beethoven's ear-trumpet at the same time*) The day before yesterday–a salami maker was painted by an artist, and therefore all painters were hauled in yesterday–no, I'm sorry, that's backward, a salami painter the day before yesterday–no, I mean the day before yesterday . . . (*continues writing silently*) In the latest work sent by the copyist there were only a few mistakes discernible when compared with the manuscripts, although in the first two movements of your large-scale new sonata I believe I've discovered strikingly many. I'm not sure about that, however, because your manuscript appears to be defective in some places, that is written with a defective pen, pure chicken scratch, so that I can't make heads or tails of it. And then all the activity in my office leaves me with very little time to spare; it's practically slave labor. I've worked my way through about half of your sonatas by now, incidentally, and would still like to request that you provide me with more specific guidance in some passages.
Beethoven:	I don't know why all my previous piano music has lately been having the most unfavorable impact on me lately, especially when it's played badly. The reason the substantial new sonata seems like chicken scratch to you, as you express it, why it seems so full of mistakes, is, in my belief, because you're afraid of it. Nothing that you're assuming to be a mistake in it *is*. You just don't think that what's there is possible.

Schindler:	Forgive me. Perhaps it's merely my nervousness. I haven't quite known recently what to do with myself or when or where. For instance, right now I need to be preparing for a set of major examinations on natural rights. But I can't just set music temporarily aside on that account, because I have a really good chance of being engaged at the Kärntnertor Theater as assistant conductor, rehearsal pianist, and chorus director.
Waldmüller:	(*to Schindler, who is still sitting next to Beethoven and is now being asked by the composer to take notes*) You spoke of natural rights, in which you have to take a series of examinations. But what do you consider natural rights to be? Could we mean a right by which nature binds itself contractually to us to fulfill certain specific obligations, noncompliance with which incurs a penalty from us? People have always maintained that natural rights exist, but inasmuch as there is no such thing as a state of nature, there can be no such thing as natural rights, because we fear nature, we wage war against it and obliterate it, thereby driving our very own selves into the ground. Rights come into existence only in what is known as a social organization or society, or, for that matter, in any given clan organization or clanship. Every state of nature, on the other hand, presupposes a human being with no constraints, entirely alone, altogether separate and discrete.
Beethoven:	(*half to himself, half to Waldmüller, while Schindler is taking notes the whole time*) So if I'm isolated, I have no rights, and no one has any rights from me–
Waldmüller:	You may make such a claim if you are also willing to fulfill it. Those are rights of yours such as

cannot eventuate in a state of nature, because in
any genuine state of nature each human being
would necessarily have to exist alone.

Beethoven: *(as previously)* But I actually do exist all alone,
perhaps as determined by my condition, and so
almost all people are neither kinship units nor
social elements to me; instead, they're nature
pure and simple, if in a certain modified sense of
the term, and they strike me more as peculiar
trees and shrubs, fully alive and walking through
the city and across country, engaged in all sorts
of preposterous activities.

Waldmüller: Rights are nothing but restrictions keeping me
from arbitrarily doing to others whatever I want
to. I am therefore entitled to demand for my part
that others observe toward me the same consideration they expect from me. Therein would lie
my rights, theoretically speaking.

Beethoven: But if there are no other persons, ones toward
whom considerations and obligations are to be
observed and from whom awaited, then all rights
come to a stop and a state of nature sets in –

Waldmüller: *(to Schindler)* But that's not in any textbook, and
you mustn't express any such thing in your ex-
aminations; I see a gloomy outcome for you if
you do.

Schindler: *(to Waldmüller)* I know how you love to make
somebody like me feel insecure, if not subject to
outright ridicule.

Beethoven: *(softly, as if to himself)*–But what if I overturned
my own natural rights even more–not just myself
and what's around me now, but also myself
alone, inside myself, which is how it's been for a
long time anyway–

Waldmüller: *(to Schindler)* Nothing could be farther from my mind than to ridicule you, and whatever it is about natural rights you're studying for your examination is pretty much mere child's play compared to some of the measures in store for us. It's being rumored that the authorities have finished drafting a law that stipulates how fast rabbits will be allowed to run and how high birds are supposed to fly.

Schindler: And what I've heard is that it's been promulgated that all the clocks in all the church steeples throughout Vienna and the surrounding region must all tell exactly the same time, starting immediately.

Beethoven: *(laughing out loud)* All the church towers here and in the general vicinity: an assemblage of monstrous Mälzel metronomes built up to the sky and actually functioning! But still operating very sporadically, sorry to say. For if the system were running correctly, the strokes from the church towers, though now marching exactly in step, would have to sound out their individual beats through the air at least once a second, but with changes of tempo precisely coordinated, first slower, then again faster, so that all pedestrians, rather than strolling along at their usual pace, only too nonchalant, as they've always done up to now, would quickly go whizzing along the sidewalks, whether of side streets or main thoroughfares, in step, marching at the identical pace, at a rate set in advance by the church-steeple metronomes, or else at a slower parade tempo; horses and carriages likewise, of course, but flocks of pigeons would also have to go fluttering to and from their perches, with their tremolized wing beats, at whatever uniform rhythm has been decided on; finally, the sky, the clouds, the daylight would all begin trembling and vibrating to the previously determined and speci-

fied tempo from the clock-tower metronomes in
such a way that soon the bridges over the river
would all start coiling and twining, up and down,
dancing across the whole width of the water, like
gigantic snakes chained to the river banks; finally, all the houses, at exactly the predetermined
rate of speed, would go staggering from one end
of the city to the other, stomping their ground
floors and cellars into the ground in movements
synchronized to the precise tempo fixed in advance by the clock-tower metronomes, while at
the same time creating syncopation by flinging
far up into the sky and then catching again, between beats, the gigantic hats of their attic floors,
thus causing displacements in the pattern of
beats—now that's something I'd really enjoy.

Waldmüller: I'd say the present state of this general chrono-
                mizing, proclaimed for and applicable to the
                whole population at large, is quite enough for
                the time being. I wouldn't even want to know
                how many clockmakers were forced to resort to
                the most complicated measures in order to fulfill
                their task with such precision and with no devia-
                tions and how many of them will be on hand to
                continue keeping this hourly prayer of the city-
                scape rising from the Vienna basin up to heaven,
                now and forever amen, with such perfect func-
                tioning, and thereby, exercising the most atten-
                tive care, to keep in smooth running order the
                clock of the entire landscape, from the western
                wetlands of the Danube to the grasslands of
                Marchfeld, from the southern foothills of the Vi-
                enna Woods all the way to the Weinviertel.
                Without smooth running order there's nothing.
                Or am I wrong? I must go now. I'll be here right
                on time for our next appointment! All the best
                until then.

*Accompanied by Schindler with his folded-up easel, Waldmüller
leaves the room.*

Beethoven: *(alone, reading carefully once more through Schindler's notes on Waldmüller's treatise concerning natural rights)*–So if I'm isolated, then I have no rights, and no one has any rights to demand of me –
– If there are indeed no other persons toward whom I have to observe and fulfill considerations and obligations, and they toward me, then all rights come to a stop and a state of nature sets in, one in which any such thing as a right is no longer possible–
– But what, then, if I were now actually to overthrow my own natural rights so as to erect them anew –
– Just as it's been a long time since I could summon the courage really to confront it –
– Even though the benefits are what I all of a sudden can make such a happy picture of in my mind–all I have to do is summon the courage and confidence so that true awareness and feeling can rise up in me, so that there might come to be in fact one of those new ways of living or manners of existence of mine, complete with all the good results it would bring –
You're not allowed to be human, though; the only happiness left for you is inside yourself, inside your art–nothing must link me to life –

(Standing up, walking around, while the computer piano begins playing the third movement of the Hammerklavier sonata very hesitantly and extremely softly.)

– And so I feel like a living, ambulatory plant whose roots, stems, leaves, and stalks are made up from the inside out of sounds growing out of the earth, sounds that appear in full bloom in my head–as good as finished, not requiring any more pruning or trimming by way of corrections –
– That's how it is that I'm already seeing the

large-scale sonata whole, even though it's not fully written out yet; it's like a picture before me,
complete from beginning to end, as if I were hearing the first and last chord at the same time, as
well as every single note, tone color, melody, and
chord in between, down to the most minute detail, in one single, brief, immeasurably fleeting
flash of a fraction of a blink sustaining itself almost ceaselessly –

*(He has gone over to his tall desk and has begun
to compose.)*

What would it be like if we could experience and
examine our lives, from birth to death, and all the
endless variety of everything in between, in all its
completeness, in a single flash, a moment so short
it would go on forever? That's probably how it will
in fact be when we finally go away from here –
– but fortunately I can let everything just unfold,
adapting itself to the prearranged tempo, with total clarity and more perfectly than it could presumably ever be played, all in exact order, so that
it's directly open to me to let it all flow out onto
the paper from my pen as I stand here at my desk

*(The computer piano continues for some time to
play the third movement of the Hammerklavier
sonata.)*

– But never before have my thoughts been able to
rise up in my brow and emerge through my face
this clearly and perfectly, but also with tender fe-
rocity, gentle rage, maniacal gentleness, serene
mania, maniacal serenity, or sweet-tempered mania; my whole body is the gigantic resonance
chamber of some instrument so perfect that it
could never even exist in theory, let alone be built,
so much so that all the musical ideas my inner ear
have produced up to now seem in comparison to
be crumbling musical mold, deteriorated and in-

fected chord clods turned rotten and foul, deathly
pale, all drained away –
– This feeling of being some kind of plant-like living being, stirred by the wind of evening and resounding, doesn't only come about when I'm
sensing and hearing the new, large-scale sonata
from first chord to last in a shorter space of time
than could ever be measured, with light rising up
in me and around me, enveloping me completely–
but also, when I am causing sounds which have
scaled the heights to the sun itself to return to
their places, all properly lined up in the right order within their units of time, that certainty that I
still am and will remain a resounding plant rooted
in this room and soaring up does not disappear,
and when I return from outside measurable time,
the very same sounds, emerging from the memory
of my soundlivingbeingexistencenature, begin
streaming out of me in an eyestorm, never mind
that my glances have begun wilting and fading
along with lightlamentsongs burning out from
overtired looking, because it all sounds more en-
thralling than anyone these days could ever produce in actual notes –

*(Beethoven sits down at the piano with great
concentration, and, without his touching the
keyboard, the computer piano again begins playing, as if out of someone's head or body, the third
movement of the Hammerklavier sonata, which
meanwhile has stopped.)*

Unfortunately, none of this can become audible to
anyone but me, not to anyone else, but I'm firmly
convinced that one day, surely in fifty or a hundred years, there will be a few talented artists who
will be capable of playing the sonata this way

*(The computer piano continues playing for a
time and then stops, while Beethoven goes back
to the table, reads the* Intelligencer, *and takes*

notes.)

– Tendler's book store in the Trattnerhof: J. A.
Danndorf, *Death and Apparent Death*, published
in Leipzig, 1816 –
– soap powder, moth balls –
– ask Schindler where he gets his knives sharp-
ened (and also what they're wearing these days in
place of an undervest) –
– large brooms, chamber pots, shovels for muck,
juniper wood –
– writing paper, pens, candles, earthenware jugs
and pots –
– at the Haarmarkt bellows made of wood only,
no leather –
– coffee cups, paper, ink, violin maker, shovels for
muck–

Schindler:	*(enters, sits next to Beethoven)* Because you have now obtained several of these new-style completely waterproof hats, you surely can't be missing that ancient felt hat of yours; besides, it's practically falling apart, so I'm taking the liberty of asking you for it as a memento, something in the nature of a relic.
Beethoven:	*(showing no reaction after having read in the notebook what Schindler has just said)* Please write to Ries in London and tell him I'll soon be mailing him a sonata that will give pianists quite a bit of trouble and that they'll be playing in fifty or a hundred years.
Schindler:	Very well, honored master, I shall draw up the letter immediately. Don't you also wish to inform Ries that you intend to dedicate to him your ninth symphony with its chorus in the last movement? Or have you reconsidered the matter in the meantime?
Beethoven:	I am now intending to offer the dedication of the symphony to the King of Prussia, who is after all the ruler of Bonn, my native city. Would you in fact be so kind as to draft a letter to this effect, addressing it to the proper official at the court chancellery in Berlin?
Schindler:	By all means. But a strange question occurs to me in this context. Is it not your belief that Goethe, even though an officially appointed minister of state, should also conduct his affairs the way a poet would? That is administer a kingdom along poetic lines, as it were? And would you then, if you were a minister of state, conduct yourself in that capacity like a composer, that is, would you administer a composition in a manner similar to the composition of a kingdom—no, administer a kingdom in a manner similar to the way in which

you strive to build the composition of your music, whatever that might mean?

Beethoven: Do you seriously believe that among all the so-called normal people, the ones who can hear—they may be serfs but they can hear the surf–a deaf person will somehow lately have acquired the status of the blind king among brow-eyed po-lyphemic titan-dwarfs?

Schindler: Forgive me, I didn't think before I asked. Let me add that I am most deeply honored by the trust you are manifesting in allowing me to help and assist in preparing the first complete edition of your works to date. But I often have the impression, I regret to say, that you should behave more cautiously in bestowing your trust. I'm thinking above all of your dealings with Holz, Oliva, or even your editor Bernard, who is always able to put you into a very happy mood, very much un-like his effect on me. What these persons are do-ing is using their appearances in public with you more to bask in the luster your shadow casts upon them. I'm always completely silent in public places, as if I were not even there. I think you need to be more suspicious of Bernard in particu-lar. His physiognomy displays, at least in my es-timation, incongruously concealed pedantry. No, I'm not being guided by prejudice here, but I would never rely on any Bohemian. One time, when we were all in a tavern by the slaughter-house, Bernard said to you in the loudest voice that the emperor is a treacherous pig who has now deceived us for the third time, and he said it almost as if he were trying to encourage those around him, including you and me as well, to make further comments and statements along the same lines, all his views appearing to arise out of a profoundly settled, stout-hearted loyalty to the court, a viewpoint so conventional it almost sounded provocative. There's still some statement of that kind somewhere in the notebooks of your conversations. You should immediately eliminate utterances of this kind from any documents of yours, either by tearing out the offending pages or at least making those passages unreadable. Imagine if those things fell into the wrong hands, especially in times like these, when the state police have started passing somewhat beyond their jurisdiction –

Beethoven: I know you're talking about Metternich's brigades of informers–those henchmen of the state police who lurk behind every public or even private toilet and consider themselves capable of detecting from all the different sounds of even the quietest flow of urine being released the basic attitude, regime-supporting or regime-toppling, of the man answering nature's call.
              If it were only possible, even remotely, to entertain hopes of happening across a single honest and upright person in the midst of this Austrian state corruption, it would be much easier to find at last a halfway suitable, tidy housekeeper. . .

Schindler: I believe I've found that honest and upright person nevertheless; yes, the right housekeeper for you may finally be within reach. In the judgment of the two women who serve me my meals, the woman is ideal and more than suitable, because she has suffered a great deal in her life, was unhappily married for fourteen years, and looks unusually neat and robust. She's a widow about forty. She's had only two posts in all that time, the last one for six years, working for the wife of a lawyer, who has informed me that the woman is the best cook who ever came her way but also doesn't get worked up about having to perform tasks like cleaning and polishing boots.
              I've explained to this person all the ways about you that are unusual, such as getting up at five in the morning, and she's more than satisfied with

| | all I've told her. She's coming tomorrow at nine-thirty to tell you when she can come. |

Beethoven: . . . whom I could for a change hold onto longer than all the rest up to now; let's say instead of one or at most two days or weeks at the most one who might stay for as long as a month or two or even for six whole months –

Schindler: To proceed now from a topic I alluded to previously, the complete edition of all your works to date (for the preparation of which you would need to focus much more time and concentration, if such a fortunate state could indeed come about) and enter onto a related proposal, for which I am trembling on the verge of presenting my humble self to you as your first biographer, I am now making so bold as to address with you in a preliminary but urgent way a point of confusion concerning your biography:
In some handbooks and encyclopedias you are persistently stated to be an illegitimate son of the most recently deceased King of Prussia, to contradict which assertion you have repeatedly been requested, most particularly by several friends from Bonn, especially for the sake of your deceased mother's honor.

Beethoven: I've heard something to that effect in passing, but I don't know any details, and I've made it a basic principle neither to write anything about myself nor to reply to anything written about me.

Schindler: Very well. There's another question—were you born in 1770, which several individuals maintain can be proven from the record, or in 1772, as others assert, yourself included?

Beethoven: (indignantly) I, Ludwig van Beethoven, was born on December 17, 1772, and every one of the allegedly accurate, though to me unequivocally erroneous baptismal certificates they've ever sent me that have December 17, 1770 as the date of birth pertain to a brother two years older and identical by name, Ludwig van Beethoven, of course, who died just after being born.

Schindler: *(embarrassed)* If I might return to an earlier matter: Because you have now obtained several of these new-style completely waterproof hats, you surely can't be missing that ancient felt hat of yours; besides, it's practically falling apart, so I'm taking the liberty of asking you for it as a memento, something in the nature of a relic.

Beethoven: *(fetching a moth-eaten hat)* That brother of mine, two years older and with the identical name, Ludwig van Beethoven, was graced with a second baptismal name, unlike myself; it was Maria, but it's altogether obvious that the responsible parties deliberately forgot to enter it onto his baptismal certificate.

Schindler: *(taking possession of the hat and leaving)* My very deep thanks to you!

Beethoven: *(reading through the* Intelligencer, *making notes
                  at times)*–Carl August Löffler, dentist on the
                  Graben, number 1160, the front staircase on the
                  fourth floor, and also Doctor Stich at Blutgasse
                  1979–The undersigned draw special attention to
                  the fact that they have acquired the skill of pro-
                  ducing on their own the newest metallic and
                  mineral teeth fashioned even in London and Par-
                  is; these are fireproof and indestructible, imper-
                  vious to all pharmaceutical preparations and ac-
                  ids–and will never change color –
                  – first speak with Staudenheimer about acids,
                  then go and ask these dentists –
                  – Ivan Simonov's *Account of the Latest Voyage
                  of Discovery to the Antarctic,* soft cover, at Wal-
                  lishauser's, Hoher Markt 453 –
                  (reading through a brochure)–In the course of
                  his experimental and empirical studies Gottfried
                  Wilhelm Leibniz discovered over a hundred years
                  ago that our hearing transmits not just certain se-
                  lected intervals but apparently most of them, if
                  not all sounds whatever, from our outer ear to
                  the eardrum, which receives the impact of every
                  oscillation audible to us and transposes each one
                  into its corresponding vibration, from which all
                  the vibrations are conducted via the inner ear
                  and the transmitting filaments of the auditory
                  nerves into the brain and its center of hearing,
                  but not as the simple sum of their frequencies;
                  instead, they are at first apprehended logarithmi-
                  cally and thus conducted ever deeper into the
                  head as the sum of the logarithms of their fre-
                  quencies, the result being that almost everything
                  we perceive and process with and in our ears by
                  way of oscillations accessible to us and accessed
                  by us is only perceivable, deep inside our heads
                  and accordingly to our own selves, as the exhaus-
                  tive dissection into each of their component parts
                  of every one of even their slightest units or de-
                  tails, subsequently recombined logarithmically

into a coherent whole –
– So then what I'm hearing of my new sonata
deep inside myself, sounding so loud and clear in
all my inner ears, isn't my sonata itself but the
sum of the logarithms of all the frequencies in the
sounds of the sonata –
– Even if my body has turned into a living, moving resonance chamber out of which I produce
the sounds of my sonata and can hear myself doing so at the same time, whether from the outside, which is impossible with my deafness, or
merely sounding from inside me through the
room, it makes no difference –
– So I've not only transformed myself into a living and moving musical instrument, my entire
body having turned into one gigantic ear, but I
am, even beyond that, the ambulatory body of my
sonata itself, in which capacity I both gestate myself acoustically and at the same time hear myself
doing so through my own organic sequencing of
the sonata and its music; I am a physically exis-
tent music being, a live one, moving freely
through this room or sitting on a chair–this one,
of course–as a visible and audible sonata life, doing just what suits me; with the help of its to-
neweftcycle, I myself have become the living,
moving, autonomously resounding, cantilena-
intelligent harmonic existence of the definitively
awakened sound individual of my sonata –
– All the life of music rising up in me is reshaping
itself, not only as if I were and would in and of
myself suddenly become this arising musical
work, which presents itself through me or I
through it in a manner true to life, meaning that
my new sonata and I match perfectly in every respect –

*(The computer piano goes on playing the third
movement of the Hammerklavier sonata by itself, as if the music were coming from Beethoven's head and body.)*

– This is not the kind of thing anyone is likely to
believe, and I have to be careful not to mention
even in the most passing way, not even to people
I trust, no matter how much, or even to friends,
anything about feelings or hints of feelings along
these lines; people would consider me to be even
more out of my mind than they already do anyway and might declare me irreversibly mentally
ill –

(The computer piano continues playing.)

The one disadvantage of having everything remain inside me without its being able to be detected outside my person –
– But with a little energy it ought to be possible
to reverse the process, as it were, by delogarith-
misizing the sonata not just from the inside of my
head and thus bringing it out of me, but also to
release my body from it and allow it to become
audible as it freely resounds for any and all music
lovers, in any space one likes, including, of
course, in the concert hall or theater –
– They would have to fasten some kind of suitable resonance chamber to my head, probably
considerable in size, strength, and projection capacity, and of course made of suitable materials –
– Although there might perhaps exist simpler solutions producing a more plausible result–for example to have them fashion trumpets even larger
than the ones attached to the tubing on my very
largest hearing devices and machines, to strap
them to my head such that the other ends lead into my ears, from which would then come streaming out from the auditory center of my brain the
delogarithmisized concentration of amassed frequencies, and the music tapped in this way would
be amplified by resonating chambers made as
easily manageable and inconspicuous as possible,
concealed as well as possible under my hair and

my clothing, all to be affixed as efficiently as possible for the purpose of concentrating attention
as much as possible on the musical work in such
a way that it can be truly delivered at maximally
appropriate volume –
– But perhaps a great deal of all this won't even
be called for and will in fact prove altogether unnecessary; everything will be easily realizable
without overly complicated contraptions, although it will require nearly superhuman effort,
the highest degree of will, and the most intense
concentration possible; but above all devotion,
the profoundest possible devotion to your destiny, because that and only that can give orders
for actions calling me to serve on this level. It's a
hard struggle, bringing everything to bear that
still must be done to make all necessary plans for
the distant journey! –
– You must find everything your sacred wishes
decree–you must wring it out of yourself by striving absolutely as your convictions dictate, always
and ever striving without arriving –

(The computer piano stops playing.)

– G. W. Leibniz, *Monadology and Theodicy*, single copies in soft covers, at Hegerleithner's, Stoss
im Himmel 526 –
– G. W. Leibniz, *The Law of Conservation of Energy and Thoughts on Unconscious Ideations*, at
the same bookstore –
– G. W. Leibniz, *New Experiments Concerning
Human Understanding*, calf-bound, or all three
works bound in a single volume, Berlin, 1715, ob-
tainable at the same bookstore –
– Leibniz definitely does not say that there is no
such thing as understanding; what he says is that
we do not know, or cannot know, what understanding is–

(Optional: The computer piano plays the section from "Largo" to "Allegro risoluto" from the fourth movement of the Ham-merklavier sonata.)

(The painter Ferdinand Waldmüller has entered to continue painting Beethoven, who is sitting to him.)

Waldmüller: *(placing the last brush strokes and scrutinizing the portrait one last time, then taking the pic-ture from the easel and holding it up in front of Beethoven to give him a good look)* The picture is finished. Look. Do you recognize yourself?

Beethoven: *cannot understand the painter and shakes his head.*

Waldmüller: *(goes over to the notebook and writes in it as he is speaking)* The picture is finished. Thank you for all your graciousness, your patience, and so on, shown by your having made time to sit to me.

Beethoven: Did I sit still enough the whole time to give your brushes time to complete the necessary strokes?

Waldmüller: Still as a tree.

               (He has again forgotten that Beethoven cannot hear, so he writes.)

               Still as a tree that doesn't move or allow itself to bend, not even in a storm.

Beethoven: A tree that never sways or makes a sound, not even in the wind? Possibly because any wind that sees it from afar avoids it? It seems to me it would be better to be the kind of tree that would sway even when there's no wind blowing, a tree whose leaves would stir because they're growing as the wings of the branches and causing their foliage, aflutter in even the most aircramped stillness, to surge and swell, because the tree is forever attempting to take off into the air.

Waldmüller: If I were standing there as the painter who is to paint that tree and then were suddenly to be struck blind, the sound of the tree in the wind would allow my ears to guide the brush with such playfulness that a great landscape painting, a storm scene frozen in motion, would emerge and rightly earn great admiration, whereas I myself would only be able to hear my picture, because in the calm of the canvas the only thing confronting me would be the surging and swaying of the tree, as if it were surf breaking against the rocky crags of a forgotten land.

Schindler: *(who has entered and is now studying the portrait)* The world will grasp him yet. It is my very happy lot to help the world along in that process through my efforts to sweep its adversities out of his way.

     (To Waldmüller, who is packing up his painting gear and preparing to leave) Don't forget the picture!

Waldmüller: *(takes the picture, takes leave of Beethoven, and, as he is going)* Of course I'll take you with me; I won't leave you alone.

Beethoven: What did he say?

Schindler: *(writes what Waldmüller said in the notebook)*

Beethoven: He's taking me with him? Tell him I don't have time to go anywhere with him, though.

Schindler: He doesn't mean you yourself; he's talking about the portrait of you.

Beethoven: Would you be so good as to write to Mälzel at
                once to say that I herewith give my binding word
                to give up all those absurd tempo markings like
                Allegro, Andante, Presto, and so forth, because
                his metronome, with its unerring march of num-
                bers not only provides me myself the opportunity
                to attain far more accurate tempos, but also be-
                cause his invention must of necessity become an
                absolute need for whole nations, and when I set
                myself at the head of a movement to achieve its
                increasing adoption, then his device will soon be
                in use in every household in Germany, Austria-
                Hungary, France, England, and so forth and will
                determine the tempo of the entire world through
                a fixed number system binding on all.

Schindler: Rhythm is indisputably the most necessary ele-
                ment for understanding in music. But in your
                works it is found mainly in nature itself. More
                and more often I take note of it in the flight of
                birds. Arsis and thesis, stressed and unstressed
                notes, on and off the beat. Don't many birds begin
                their flight on an upbeat, with an accent? The fal-
                con, for example, or the eagle—

Beethoven: Yes indeed, the eagle, the vulture, and all those
                kinds of dull-witted, plump waterfowl —

Schindler: Yes, waterfowl, and I'm happy that you think I'm
                right. Many another kind takes off with a drop in-
                stead of an upbeat, though. I'm thinking of swifts;
                after their soaring flights into the heights of the
                firmament they either come plummeting out of
                the sky, all at the same time, like a chorus in
                flight, beginning with the single mighty swooping
                drop, off the beat, of a long-drawn, expansive
                chord adrift through the air or with countlessly
                many and varied curving drops and as many
                markings of the beat for countless isolated varia-
                tions, hurtling downward, each bird floating
                earthward on its own.

Beethoven: *(as if he were looking through the* Intelligencer*)–*
I've just now happened on an advertisement here
for something that might furnish you with additional study material: *The Lives of Wood Wasps,
Stag Beetles, and Glowworms,* observed by Con-
rad Florenzer, with hand-colored illustrations,
pigskin-bound, available at Kuchelschäb and
Kammerjäger's, formerly Bettenwanzer and Milb
on Höllenpfortsdampfstossgasse, next to the
"Rust-Red Chimney-Sweep" tavern.
By the way, Diabelli had sent to me just recently a
totally inept little patchwork scrap with a request
enclosed for me to write a variation on it and send
it to him. He's also gone ahead and had the same
ratty, threadbare musical rag sent to every other
living composer with an appeal identically
worded; then he proposes to gather them together
and publish them as "a" work, if not as "his" work.
But the more slugglishly this pathetic, rickety little waltz cripple tries to jump up into my face, the
more keenly I feel inclined to concoct not just one
variation for Diabelli, but to send a whole flock of
wheeling, soaring variation-birds whooshing
around his head and swooping around his ears. In
fact, I've already thought out a couple of these
whirling feathered-friend miniatures, all motley
and particolored, and if you have no objection, I
would like to perform one or two examples of
these wingèd beings in sound –

*Schindler nods with enthusiastic agreement. Beethoven mean-
while fastens around his head a huge frame with two monstrous trumpets jutting out of his ears; the way it looks lends it
almost the character of a sarcastic crown, though it also con-
veys a beauty that is more than just ironic and sarcastic. He
takes a seat at the computer piano, from which is heard Variation 10 of the Diabelli Variations, op. 120, though Beethoven's
fingers of course never touch the keys, which don't find contact
necessary anyway, because the composer knows, after all, that
the music is resounding out of himself, out of his body, and es-*

*pecially out of his head through the enormous sound trumpets,
as can be heard clearly, brilliantly, and dazzingly from the
computer piano, playing on its own, while Schindler has remained seated stage rear, at the table by the window, and the
composer laughs out boomingly from time to time and stomps
the rhythm on the floor with his feet while the tenth variation is
playing.*

Beethoven:	*(after the music has come to an end, still laugh-ing)* So what do you think of this shimmering, wing-sound fluttering tremolo-hoopoe that's at-tempting to hammer and pound a nest into Dia-belli's ears and other orifices, almost like a woodpecker, with its elongated beak?
Schindler:	*(going over to Beethoven with the notebook)* I beg your pardon, dear master, but I don't quite understand. What is it I'm supposed to have just heard? You're surely trying to pull my leg again, as you've done rather often in the form of creat-ing some sort of endearing satire on the spur of the moment.
Beethoven:	*(suddenly very serious)* What do you mean? I don't quite understand either. I think it would be best if you now left my house for a time and stayed away from me for longer than usual.
Schindler:	Of course I would be happy to leave immediately, since that is your wish, because I've always un-derstood that I need to leave you in peace when you need to be alone. However, I must with regret insist on discussing with you a matter of urgency, one that cannot be postponed, as it concerns your safety, your health, and your very life–I'm utterly appalled at what was recently inflicted on you in Wiener Neustadt. That must have caused you night-mares!
Beethoven:	*shakes his head very decidedly and grumbles*

something that can't be understood.

Schindler:	No, you say? You surely don't mean to say that it was all a pleasant experience for you? I simply can't believe that. We've already spoken about how you should travel by yourself as little as possible, rarely in fact, because of the calamity with your hearing. More particularly when it's a matter not of one-day trips but longer outings, two-day or several-day excursions through the countryside, even if they should be in areas you're familiar with. Even in places you know, you could make your way into an isolated stretch of country and suddenly not be able to find your way back.
Beethoven:	Are you saying that an area which one minute previously I knew like my old slippers could suddenly be obliterated from my memory the very next second so that I wouldn't even know where I am—as if I could start wandering around lost here in my own room –
Schindler:	All I really want to say is that if even your dearest friends Oliva, Holz, and of course Bernard can't find the time to keep you company on your little outings through the region, you might then want to call on me, since I will always find a way somehow to be on hand. But there's one thing I request with utmost fervor: Please do not ever travel to Wiener Neustadt again! Promise me that!
Beethoven:	*grumbles with furious refusal.*
Schindler:	If you nevertheless absolutely must go there again, then please let me go along, so that you don't meet with any new mishap!
Beethoven:	*(with ill temper)* And just what kind of mishap am I supposed to meet with there of all places?

Schindler: Are you now actually going to maintain that you
               weren't placed under arrest and locked up in the
               most brutal way by the Wiener Neustadt police?
               Like some kind of a vagabond or even like some-
               one who has made himself politically suspect, be-
               cause you looked into the windows of all the
               houses, even though you didn't know any of the
               people, just as you sometimes do here in Vienna?

Beethoven: *(grumbling incomprehensibly)*–Oh, that's what
               you mean.

Schindler: And because you got into a furious wrangle with
               every waiter you happened upon in every wine
               tavern and restaurant about the price of every
               single scrap of bread, which is also how you
               sometimes behave here in Vienna –
               In several other taverns you allegedly demanded
               the check at once but had hardly even entered the
               place, had just that second come in from outside;
               or you instantly insisted, *stante pede*, even to the
               point of threatening when ignored, on paying up
               without having consumed or drunk anything at
               all.

Beethoven: – I did? –

Schindler: *(growing more and more agitated and writing
               less and less in the notebook)* You went through
               the streets of Wiener Neustadt gesticulating wild-
               ly and yelling so loudly that the term they wrote
               down for your behavior was "bellowing and
               shouting"; then you often talked to yourself, hold-
               ing long speeches, delivering to yourself while
               standing still harangues of your own composition.
               On the part of the officers of the law there was
               pronounced a suspicion of unconcealed public ac-
               tivity injurious to the state, and they supposedly
               even attempted as a further precautionary secu-
               rity measure to saddle you with a charge of high

treason based on how you had pulled your totally
beat-up and crumpled-up floppy hat all the way
over your head and as far down over your face as
possible, how your overcoat, much too large, was
sweeping the cobblestones, and how you kept
switching back and forth from the double lor-
gnette perched on your nose to a monocle you
likewise kept taking on and off, while at the same
time—oh yes, it's something you're well known for
here in Vienna, something the Viennese would
even come to miss if it suddenly stopped—pacing
back and forth in front of the Imperial and Royal
Barracks of the Wiener Neustadt Military Academy, not of course without humming and suddenly shouting at the top of your lungs while
stomping with your feet and making mysterious
entries in the notebook you kept secretly taking
out.
And to think that, at the police station, even before you were taken off and locked up in the jail
there, they took from you and formally im-
pounded the very notebook of your conversations
in which the emperor is referred to as a treacherous pig, and which, it's only too easy to imagine,
could well be subjected to intense scrutiny by
Metternich's authorities, the result of which for
me could be that my prospective position as first
musical director at the Kärntnertor Theater might
well go up in smoke, inasmuch as that remark is
very close on the page to something I said and
noted in my own handwriting, something entirely
innocuous, but nevertheless –
And if you hadn't constantly stormed and yelled
in jail and in that way succeeded, by persistently
repeating the name of a school master you knew
in passing there in Wiener Neustadt, a man who
knew who you were and thus could prove your
identity, in getting them to decide at last to go
and fetch the one man there who was actually in a
position to explain to the people whom they were
in fact dealing with, you might very well have

been locked away in the madhouse, where you
would still be today, if not for the rest of your life,
because the insane idea that you might have gone
off to Wiener Neustadt would not have occurred
to anyone here, meaning that it could never have
entered anyone's mind to look for you there, no
matter how long you might have been gone!
So please, take me with you the next time you
venture to Wiener Neustadt, if you absolutely
must go there, that is, so that I can guard against
all that, even if I couldn't prevent any of it at the
time!

Beethoven: And what is it you believe you might have been
able to prevent? Do you perhaps think I might
have exhibited different behavior in your presence, behavior about which, by the way, I could
not at the time and still today cannot find anything markedly unusual? It's quite possible you
might have been arrested along with me, and indeed if you had not been known to that school
master—as of course you in fact would not have
been—you would probably have had to remain in
jail, which is where the direst mishaps would
have come about for me in my efforts to get you
back out of there; accordingly you would not be
the one having so much trouble over me, but I
over you instead. So it's clearly much better that
you didn't go with me, and it will be better for
you also to stay at home the next time I take a
trip to Wiener Neustadt, which I am confidently
assuming I will do within the next couple of days,
or at the latest next week, if not perhaps as soon
as tomorrow.
Incidentally, have you finally set a firm date for
my academy? As one who is in process of emerging as one of the more authoritative conductors
at the Kärntnertor Theater you will surely be able
to assert yourself and get results, won't you?
Have you not also read what several foreign
journals have repeatedly been lamenting in ref-

erence to my person lately? They're saying I've
been forgotten here in Vienna, even though I've
been here in Vienna the whole time.
Or is it more—as explained to me recently by an
outstanding musician from abroad who is not
prepared at any price to appear under the circumstances prevailing at the moment here—that
compositional skill is no longer understood here
in Vienna and that it's the fault of theater audiences?

Schindler: You're not imagining things. Preparations and
rehearsals always turn out these days to be much
more difficult than they used to be. It's always the
singers, too; they bail out because their part presents their vocal apparatus with difficulties
they're just not up to. Others find their parts not
sufficiently rewarding or attractive or consider
them too rigorously conceived and thus unsin-
gable—those latter are of course hiding their failure behind claims like that. Then all the chorus
members begin complaining that their line is unreachably high and they have to scream their
throats raw and hoarse instead of being able to
give their all to sing the line properly.
Even so, I can give you this much of an affirma-
tion today—the next definite date will to all appearances not be longer than a week from now,
two weeks at the most, or perhaps a month or two
months, subject to postponement by six months
or a year. We've been granted better luck with our
most recent staffing than we've had for a long
time.
Soon, then, within a few weeks, it will be definite.
You can start looking forward to it; all those involved in the performance will give everything
they've got, if not even more.
We would also like to ask you with all our hearts
to attend a few of the rehearsals when they're farther along, if you wish; that would be an energizing stimulus for us, a true honor.

Beethoven: Well, of course. Gladly. As soon as I can. And if
                  the state of my health permits. As far as the or-
                  ganization of the program is concerned, it proba-
                  bly should remain as we've spoken about since
                  the beginning, with the items in the same order,
                  so that way I can hardly imagine any problems
                  arising. As we arranged, we will begin with the
                  overture to *The Consecration of the House*, to be
                  followed, but a bit later in the program than I en-
                  visioned at first, as I just recently decided, by the
                  Ruins of Athens, and, as it stands at the moment,
                  that is tentatively, the crowning finale will be the
                  large-scale cantata *The Glorious Moment*.

Schindler: Why are you suddenly talking about a "tentative"
                  order of the program, whereas we were dealing all
                  along with an order as good as fixed for good, and
                  not just by me alone? I'm not the only person
                  you're making uneasy by now, at the very last
                  moment, beginning to contemplate possible
                  changes. Any adjustment at all, small in scope as
                  well as large, would not only be unworkable for
                  everyone involved; it would be a disaster! Now of
                  all times, when everything is running solidly and
                  smoothly along the paths laid out, you want to
                  change something? Well, what then? You're mak-
                  ing me very perplexed!

Beethoven: The small program change I have in mind
                  needn't upset you, because it effects you neither
                  as the administrator supervising the preparations
                  nor as the conductor; it concerns me and me
                  alone.

Schindler: And how so, please?

Beethoven: Let me explain and also request you to see to the
                  very modest arrangements necessary. What I
                  would like is for the orchestra temporarily either
                  to leave the podium altogether after the overture

or for the musicians to shift as far as possible off
to the sides and to the rear, so that the platform
will be largely free; then the best available concert piano should be placed onto the proscenium
in such a way that the keyboard is entirely turned
away from the audience's view, its rear facing the
listeners head on.

Schindler: And why all that?! Why?!

Beethoven: Because I want to—and I shall—insert at this point
in the program the large-scale sonata I've just recently completed—of course you know very well
which one I mean—and, by undergoing the ordeal
of appearing for the last time as pianist—
reluctantly, at that, as I'm sure you can and indeed must believe—will perform it for my public,
in person, entrusting it to no one else; not to
make myself important, but because I have no
choice. I feel called upon to play my most important sonata to date at least this one time, which
will perhaps be the only time and the last time as
well, in the way it really has to be played, because
I know perfectly well that this is a sonata which
will, at the very least, not be heard again for a
very, very long time, for whatever reasons.

Schindler: *(frozen in horror)* Earlier I thought and said that
the world will grasp you yet and that it is my very
happy lot to help the world along in that process
through my efforts to sweep its adversities out of
your way, but now you want to grasp the world,
seize hold of it in a destructive way, and it is now
my very unhappy lot to sweep the adversities you
cause out of its way.

Beethoven: You're appalled, I can see that, but it makes no
difference and changes nothing.

Schindler: *(completely losing his composure, writing almost nothing in the notebook now, and collaps-*

ing) I'm not merely appalled; I'm totally shattered, horrified, outraged, and shocked, and I
protest! Mainly because of you, when all is said
and done, and along with you, to some extent, because after all it's you who have always dragged
me into your schemes and are still doing so, for
that matter, I feel utterly ruined, as good as
smashed to pieces and lying on the ground completely destroyed! How do you think you're going
to get out of this situation even partway un-
scathed? Or don't you even want to? You yourself
know better than anyone that as a result of your
total deafness there is practically nothing remaining of the virtuosity people so admired earlier in
your playing. At every forte passage you flail away
so violently at the keys that the strings not only
buzz, they snap. When the passage is piano or
pianissimo, by contrast, your fingers don't even
make contact with the keys most of the time, so
there's nothing to hear. And because you almost
never play any more, either in public or in private, let alone practicing, your former dexterity
has vanished altogether. But yet and still you're
proposing not only to make a public appearance
performing what I consider to be your most difficult and complex piano work, but, you're more-
over upholding the supposition, alien to all reality, that you and you alone are capable of executing your work such that it thereupon becomes
your artistic duty to do so, whereas this work will
never ever be able to be played, not by anyone! I
can only have the deepest pity for you! And then
all your peculiar antics while playing–sticks
clenched between your teeth and dangling down
into the piano so that you can pick up whatever
vibrations in your head, and then the strange
contraptions you call your hearing machines that
you insist on strapping to and around your head,
by which I understand you to be trying to withdraw from the piano keyboard and from the view
of the audience. This event will prove to be the

saddest and most tragic final appearance of the
greatest artist the world has ever seen, and all
those who love you and have always loved you to
idolatry will mourn and lament your appalling
decline and fall; it goes without saying, too, that
some will not be able to refrain from heaping savage contempt on you, the fault for which will be
entirely yours and will turn you into the most pathetic fool ever!

Beethoven: None of the circumstances connected with any
matter I've thought about so thoroughly could be
more vividly present to anyone more than to myself. Do you really believe I would undertake to
present my most important sonata if it were all
going to turn out the way you're painting it? Do
you then believe I am so far removed from all
power of judgment as not to know what I should
be doing and not doing? Do you consider me one
who was once upon a time a great artist but is
now capable only of insane actions and therefore
needs to be placed under the watchful eye of a
keeper such as yourself?
So now, if we can go by outward appearance, you
seem a little calmer than earlier, and to soothe
your agitation even more, to allow you to see for
yourself that I am very well capable of performing the sonata before an audience, and in the
manner I've made provision for, I will play it for
you right now, at least some excerpts. Come here!
Sit down over there! Just wait and listen! *(To
himself)* Let everything called life be sacrificed to
unadulterated greatness; let it become the holi-
ness of art; let me live, even if I have to be helped
along by whatever resources I can find!

*Schindler sits at the table by the window. Beethoven sits at the
piano and makes as if he were playing. The computer piano
plays from the first movement of the Hammerklavier sonata,
from the development section through the reprise and to the*

end, as if the music were sounding out of Beethoven's head and body.

Beethoven: *(after the playing has stopped)* Are you now
                  convinced, at least to some degree, that every-
                  thing will work out for the best?

Schindler: *(very puzzled and bemused, still completely
                  bowled over from his previous outburst, not
                  writing the following in the notebook)* Well, I re-
                  ally can't think of anything to say. Not to you. Not
                  to the wall. Not even to the window. Did you play
                  something? I don't know what and can't tell what
                  there was for me to hear. You'll know best what I
                  mean. I watched you with great pleasure. You
                  would seem to have played an immensely mas-
                  sive, strong piece, as I could see, and I'm totally
                  bowled over by it. Several of the chords seemed to
                  be slapping me in the face with their large hands,
                  as if you wanted them to wake me out of a swoon.

Beethoven: You still have not recovered your composure, and
                  that makes me feel sorry for you. Probably still
                  exhausted from all the excitement earlier. Now I
                  will play you something from the slow move-
                  ment. That will help you regain your balance.

*The computer piano plays the third movement of the Hammerk-
lavier sonata to the end. Same situation as previously.*

Schindler: *(sometimes getting up for a second and looking
                  at the composer, who appears to be playing)*
                  There's almost nothing to hear, but some kind of
                  sound is getting into my head anyway—no, now
                  there's nothing again. But it's totally distinct even
                  so, making a loud noise, but in some inexplicable
                  way it's not here in the room, but more as if it
                  were being conveyed directly from his head into
                  my body, without the sounds having to make
                  their way through the air first. Louder and louder
                  now, very distinct, too, and yet almost as if it

were sounding somewhere outside the room, beyond space itself, even though I am in this room
and can hear with exceptional clarity, so no, it has
to be in this room and sounding here. But now all
of a sudden almost nothing again–

Beethoven: *(after the third movement has come to an end)*
               How do you like that? And don't say it was
               played badly!

Schindler: *(still perplexed and annoyed, but, in a manner
               disconcerting to himself, also thrilled and skepti-
               cally fascinated all at the same time; sitting next
               to Beethoven at the piano and writing the follow-
               ing in the notebook, though only bits and pieces
               of it)* It was wonderful somehow. Often so quiet I
               didn't think I was hearing anything. Just your
               breath. I could read the deepest of feelings in
               your face. What we have here is music that seems
               hardly to be composed of sounds any more, music
               in which you have seemingly found a way more of
               crafting all the different gradations of silence and
               quietness in the most highly musical and per-
               fectly wrought way, almost as though you no
               longer required sound in order to give music
               shape. Only I wonder if the people, the audience,
               that is, will understand what you've done.

Beethoven: How do you mean that?

Schindler: Well, I don't know if people will understand a si-
               lence wrought with such absolute mastery of
               craft, a soundlessness worked to such rigorous
               perfection; in short, a piece that can be compre-
               hended only with utmost concentration.

Beethoven: If people will understand, you ask? Well now, the
               way for me to remove your lingering doubt is
               through the great closing fugue.

Schindler again sits at the table by the window, standing up at times in his attempts to watch Beethoven's fingers more closely, while the computer piano plays the great closing fugue up to the "Sempre dolce" marking.

Beethoven: I'll spare myself the rest; my head's already about to explode. This work belongs in the large concert hall, not in a small room like this one – – What's that you're saying now? This will fill the theater with more sound than the orchestra before it, don't you think?

Schindler: No.

Beethoven: Excuse me?

Schindler: I couldn't hear anything. I don't even know what you're saying. Not a note of music, although that's all you're talking about.

Beethoven: So which one of us is the deaf one? You or me? Could you by any chance have temporarily lost your hearing all of a sudden, just a few minutes ago, whereas I, the one who's almost completely unable to hear, have suddenly heard everything splendidly? I have seldom heard music more clearly and with much more focused precision. So are you the one who's deaf, or am I? In any case, I heard perfectly well, and anyone else could have heard it just as well.

Schindler: *(says each of the following sentences a few times, one by one, before he writes them down in the notebook, as if he were trying to test and demonstrate Beethoven's hearing ability)* So you heard everything, did you?! But now you can't hear anything I'm trying to say to you, for example; instead, I have to write it all down for you to read. Why is it that you don't hear anything I say, not a word of anything I try so strenuously to explain to you? Or is it that you don't want to hear?

Beethoven: Now you're turning arrogant, too! You must realize that I can't let myself be treated that way. Or
at least you should realize that I won't stand for
your coming at me with that scheming and plotting brand of bad taste that's all your own, a trait
you quite like and even find irresistible, for that
matter; don't try your overwhelmingly generous
capacity for defamation, delivered in your own
inimitably pompous yet pipsqueaky loud-
mouthed style on me; keep your loud-mouthed
littleness to yourself. And here's something I've
not only suspected but actually known for a long
time—you are a totally lowdown, stout-heartedly
treacherous, calculating, gag-reflex-activating,
phony son of a bitch! And look at how you found
ways and means of crawling into my life with
such ever-so-courteous, outrageous impudence!
With an unbelievable fervor you should be morti-
fied to contemplate, if you had any shame,
tricked out as an affable, obliging manner entirely in the service of benefiting me enormously,
you always found it easy, in your shallow and
open but deep and secret directness, to pass off
all your activities as efforts to shield me from the
world, whereas all the while you were treacher-
ously exercising your self-proclaimed, self-
sacrificial willingness to help, seamy and self-
serving and outright obstructive as it was, for the
furtherance of your own affairs.
Until you reached the point of getting me to en-
dorse you as my biographer, however peculiar
the choice, which you succeeded in bringing
about on the basis of an arrogant reserve and a
reserved arrogance, often masquerading, with
full intent, as charmingly awkward reticence,
which you then used, bolstered by that gawky refinement of yours, to snoop and pry, if not actually to spy, into my business on a regular basis by
finding ways and means of turning around every
one of my suspicions—all of them long-standing,

by the way–and extracting yet more trust from
me. Of course your more than obvious, preten-
tiously modest behavior should have been
enough reason for me to unmask you long ago,
all the more because there were only too many
signs of your having already reduced me to a character from your forthcoming book, a figure you
can deploy at your whim through the streets of
Vienna, a source of rapt and fascinating embar-
rassment, from now on, that is, merely an item in
a life seemingly my own but in reality fabricated
by you and hence fixed for all time to come as a
lie. But now you have finally shown exactly who it
is I'm in fact forced to deal with. And from a person endowed with such a wealth of stunted emotions and such high-flying mediocrity of musicianship the music you just now heard must necessarily be withheld, must remain beyond said
person's reach. Given the utter ordinariness so
exceptionally deep-seated in your very character,
it can never have been short of outright impossible for you to grasp anything extraordinary. That
is why you chose not to hear a note of what was
played and why you acted toward me as if you
had not heard anything; with great force of concentration, helped along by your enthusiastically
enthralled power of rejection, you may indeed
have succeeded in deflecting every note.
More than likely, though, you're simply pretending to have heard nothing, because your main
concern is to prevent me from actually performing the sonata in public at the academy, since you
not only are afraid of my appearing personally to
play that piece but also since you fancy yourself
and pet projects, *The Consecration of the House*
and *The Glorious Moment*, to be in grave danger.
And you might not be so wrong at that, since
your house blessing and your moment of glory
could indeed start wobbling quite seriously the
minute I enter with my supposed hearing machine screwed together and strapped to my head;

I freely admit it oversteps into the realm of immensity all previous dimensions, external proportions, and orders of magnitude, and wearing it is anything but a pleasure, I can tell you, for it does not, as many think, serve to improve my hearing, but rather to allow the piece of music that I myself am to penetrate its way from the inside of me to the outside, having so completely turned my whole self into music that I can go on living as I should only as that music and as nothing else. However, I am hampered in my efforts to elucidate further in anything even approaching a scientific manner as much by the almost brilliant pettiness of your virtuosically stupified oafish intelligence as by the circumstance, much more significant as far as I'm concerned, that none of this is any of your business, not yours or anyone else's, either. So don't give another thought to any of these matters, including your *Consecration of the House* or *Glorious Moment*. You needn't worry; you won't have any more problems with me, because I am herewith, right now, cancelling the academy. Put a stop to any preparations in progress. If I had my way, I would also prohibit you permanently from playing in your own home any of my earlier sonatas, which could at best only come out as pathetic little compost heaps of sound made of the most repulsive pianistic excremental exudings produced by a noble instrument fallen victim to your mistreatment. That's outside the realm of possibility for me, though. I do forbid you, on the other hand, from ever again bringing any work of mine to performance before the public. Not only is this particular concert withdrawn and cancelled, but there will be no dealings between us whatever in the future. I hope not to have to come upon you ever again, not here or anywhere else.
Now pack up everythingthing of yours that's still here and clear out! Whatever of mine is at your home you can send in a cart. Do not take it upon

yourself ever to turn up in person here again. If you did, I would take aim directly above your head at exactly the right moment, even before you finished climbing the stairs, and open the seat of my pants, in that way coming to the aid of the building by discharging back out onto the street with utmost dispatch the excrement that is your paltry, groveling, slithering figure, for which meritorious action the very walls of this building, however crumbly and decayed by the constant wetness of mortar forever saturated with piss, would feel most deeply indebted to me!

Schindler has been gathering up his belongings as quickly as he can and now takes to his heels.

Beethoven: Of course I will perform the sonata in public at the earliest possible opportunity; but once only; nothing will sway me from that. And if it should indeed prove true that it's not possible for me to introduce a piece of well-composed music in Vienna because people are intriguing against me, then I'll take it, if I must, to Wiener Neustadt. Or even to Sankt Pölten.

It's unfortunate that I'll have to subject the audience to all my antics, to act as if I were actually playing the piano, although I have no need whatever of that. But if I didn't cavort, people would judge a process which has become entirely second nature to me as witchcraft. The audience would not be able to understand any of it, nor would they have any understanding for me if I did not make a great show of being busily occupied at the keyboard. I assume, in fact, that it has always been necessary, at all times and in all places, to put on some kind of an act for the audience about something that has no reality, because otherwise people would pay no heed to anything an artist produces. But if I go through all that, they'll now be able to hear the sonata with a degree of comprehension that will otherwise not be available for

at least fifty or a hundred more years. All my buffoonish antics are a fair price to pay if I can make
that happen.
– Or if I could summon up the courage to do it
without all that carrying on. There is much to be
done on earth; do it soon. Perhaps art is demanding this very sacrifice. I take a seat on the platform, preferably with no piano there, or on a chair
beside the piano, and simply allow the sonata to
resound for the audience in the hall the way it
really is and the way I really am: a completely independent, autonomously moving being, alive, existing only with, in, and for my soundorgan-
ismharmonycirculatorysystem, defying any and
all weather conditions and prevailing circumstances of climate, made of sound and sound only
as I pour out the music of my Hammerklavier-
sonatabody; then perhaps the people sitting out
there in the hall will believe they are at times
hardly able to see me sitting on a chair up on the
podium, if they can see at all, because, right in
front of their eyes, I will have rarified or vapor-
ized, resolved into light dances and shadow harmony emotions of sound feelings and nervefila-
ment cantilenas of narrativemelodic chordcon-
catenated organs, my body rendered audible by
the acoustical anatomy of my sonata figure.
All of them will hear it, marvel, and grow confused
and upset, but heartened as well, perhaps. But if
only such people are sitting in the audience from
whom no understanding or feeling can be drawn,
then I would be happy just to withdraw from the
scene. To depart so that no one would notice by
letting myself just drift out from the concert hall
in the form of a fading sonata echo, floating outward from the city and out into the countryside,
resounding still across the continent and away.
Completely alone, or with my nephew and no one
else, provided I can by then get him out of the
clutches of the Queen of the Night–to England, to
one of the remote islands of the Hebrides, where

we can be all alone and make a whole new start,
everything different. But only if he really wants to.
If he doesn't want to, which I'm sure he won't,
then let him stay here with the Queen of the
Night.
Then I'll go to the Hebrides by myself.
From there, I would find a way of having all the
pieces not yet composed delivered to someone
here, some reliable person who would then be so
painstaking and accurate in overseeing further
developments that everyone would think they
were dealing with me personally.
In the Hebrides I will spend long days and weeks
listening with such minute attention to the earth
and the sun, their stories and the music of their
stories, that I will one day, little by little, have
turned matters around and at last brought our
planet and our sun to the point of listening with
equally minute attention to me and my music.
In grave and fanatical heights of blithehearted ir-
ritability
altogether merryminded weeping and wailing
filled with sadness at its most pleasurable
melancholy agreeableness
entangled in pitiable bliss
hopelessly redeemed
in euphoric somberness
restricted by the ridigidy of cautiously chaotic order
perfectly acute clarity of vision returning to the
wild in the gentle fury of the most lovingminded
deeds of violence
that vision marked by stark raving madness that
will provisionally save everyone and everything
yet one more time
ceaselessly driven hither and yon while sunk deep
in sleep restlessly tirelessly paralyzed
in comatose wideawake alert gales of grief laughter
equable and well-balanced in a jollitydepression
and depressionjollity prudently confused alto-

gether –

*(The computer piano has begun playing the
fugue again, beginning with the "Sempre dolce"
marking and going to the end of the sonata.)*

*(Optional: During Beethoven's closing monologue, there may be
several indications that he has little by little been breathing not
just the air, but also the light around him, by which means—as a
result, that is, of the dusk he is exhaling from his lungs—a gathering darkness soon begins flooding the entire space with a
blackness that little by little reaches all the way up. But as the
intensity of the double fugue increases all the light that had disappeared into and with the composer now somehow emerges
again, as if from the computer piano or some other source until,
by the closing chord at the latest, everything is drowned in a
spreading brightness downright painful to the eyes.)*

BLINDING MOMENT:

THE DEATH OF ANTON WEBERN

A NOVELLA

In September 1945
Doctor Anton Webern
was shot by U. S. Army cook
R. N. Bell, who died
in September 1955

Slow down, Raymond; drink slower so you'll have some left for later!
To hold up to your eyes, right now, in addition to black pictures in which not much remains visible, those black overpaintings with remnants of other pictures around the edges, thus to thrust you deep into the distance of some beyond, crumbled remains of your formerhood, whose imminent vanishing in the unconscious could only seem fine to you by this time.
Careful, any second your pupils are going to start squeezing down tighter and tighter on every light beam thrusting inward, until the throats of them all are throttled and their suffocated threads of light deposit across your entire eye a viscous coating of gummy, flabbed-out, bleary sunbeams, your glance at any given time accordingly encompassing only as a clogged vista every unperturbed outlook onto an already determined futurehood filled with enticing temptations that make it bearable to you, but then, at once, by way of inescapable conclusion, onto a futurehood with something totally alien and remote from you and your life story, flying toward you more as though from a future neverhood rendered entirely remote, interim of twilight that actually never even comes your way, your body, by way of inescapable conclusion, standing still in front of you for a long time, left behind by you and everyone else, yes, Raymond, standing still for a long, long time, no doubt as if set in place at that one spot from now on, or rather secured there already, that evening twilight prevailing on that 13th of September 1945, that first belated windfall

postwar summer day, you in the back seat of a jeep behind your
commanding officer, Captain Murray, who has just ordered the
driver next to him to start out from the village through the prevailing evening mist of autumn, after you, just a short time before, left the jam-packed dance hall next door to the inn, the
sweatsmelling steamhaze of whose misty, vaporous cloudcon-
densations you've just barely, with foot-dragging, been able to
get away from, pursued by the dance-band music sound on the
chordstench whine of a wind blowing past you as you went into
the inn this evening, lifted into your arms the cardboard cartons
heavy-laden with black-market groceries, and reached the jeep
just as it was driving away.

In that inn, the largest building in the area, the command staff of
Rainbow Company and the command staff of the army of occu-
pation have set up their headquarters and have now invited the
residents of the village to join the soldiers in the dance hall next
door for a harvest festival, as it's called, and this party hall, temporarily slapped together out of lumber and leaning up against
the other building, was on the point of bursting through its own
wooden walls and collapsing, oh yes indeed, this delirious wood-
en hut has gone stark raving mad, hopping up and down insanely
and bellowing out of its chimney, as if it wanted to break loose
from the walls of the inn, so that some general, already plastered,
is promising to open fire on this drunked-up dog house, using
tanks he's threatening to call any minute now; this was the first
time in his life the general had ever seen a building that was
completely drunk, yes indeed, a structure all boozed up and bab-
bling, belching out of its every window, as he's said to have told it
later on.

Slow down, Raymond, drink slower so you'll have some left for
later!

Black-market operators aren't supposed to be staggering as they
go about their shady transactions, not even when, as in your case
now, every step your body takes in a different direction at any
given moment could be your last one, even though with you it's a
matter of having to suffer through a whole decade till the end of
your life.

You know, Raymond Norwood Bell, almost all people have a totally false idea of their life expectancy, most of them probably
never more than when it comes to dying, for they believe totally
as a matter of course that at the final point of a completed existence everything will go rapidly flashing past them, although it's
none other than this latter view that's more false than any other
assertion advanced about the end. Many require not one instant
more than ten minutes until they're dead, or even just ten seconds, Raymond, but there are others who need ten years, because they start dying a long time before their death, hanging
suspended at some point in a life of theirs that wasn't even up to
them and that never again comes their way, trapped in a blinding
moment that seeps away—and not only as in that house over
there—up ahead.

Put down the bottle and pick up the cartons; follow Captain Murray, who's already gone ahead so he could enter the kitchen of
that house by the back door; you already know the people there;
everything's taken care of in quick order; no sooner in the kitch-
en than you meet that man toward whom a certain mistrust always seemed appropriate, and you reluctantly set the two boxes
of tropical fruit in front of him on the kitchen table, not yet
cleared of the family dinner, at which point the woman from Matell's is at once handing your captain the money—good that they
both want to have it over and done with quickly today.

Did this really have to be—a crunching sound coming in through
the window, footsteps approaching over sand and gravel, then
moving away, and Captain Murray orders you to head outside at
once, as quick as you can, to take a look, to see whose footsteps
have been following this black-market transaction with obviously
hostile intent.

Slow down, Raymond, nice and slow along the corridor, give
yourself really lots of time, keep in mind that you've still got ten
whole years left to walk along the corridor and out to the front of
the house.

At the arch of the doorway the old man, free of his own shadow,
inside which he had hidden himself up until now—or had he re-

solutely pushed his shadow away, off to the side, so he could finally stand before you in such clear view—but then again gro-
tesquely wrapped around himself, turned sideways toward one of
his pants pockets, looking for a match now, his figure so skewed
in the process that his body is wrapped practically all the way
around his shadow and back again, his fingers holding the sulfur
head of the match he had been so intently searching for, striking
it on some rough surface in midair, thereupon a hysterical
screech of laughter from the match, met by a head bowed aslant
over the rather dark area over the illuminated match, bobbing
down toward the flame; but no, it's not his head that's bobbing,
because just now the cigar dangling from his lips is coming into
view, gently waving as it is immersed in the flame and remains
immersed, long and thoroughly, so it can undergo an illumination of utmost lovingness, until the burned-out match goes tumbling to the ground.

Thereupon an echo of light falls onto the old man's face, out of
which an age-marked smile is released most suddenly and, with
an age-marked smile, shatters to pieces on you while inbound into your own face, though it seems, astoundingly—as, in coming
toward you, it slaps you in its age-marked way in the face, such
that it can only have been your own face—to be your own laughter, a laughter ahead of its time about a future that cannot possibly ever be yours, too far ahead of its time for it ever to happen to
you, fallen back into your face, so that the wall of your face, supposedly still young, marks herewith—by an inexplicable rise of
temperature attendant on the process (which glows brightly as it
keeps coming at you) of growing marked by age—your own age-
marked state of being laughed at in the assault-style attack of ar-
son hurtling at you this moment, the waves of heat from which
commence burning away and then in fact finish burning away
from your age-old face, yet more age-marked by the grimacing of
the flames coming your way, your face as it is at the moment, until you feel that the wall of your young face is turning into a cliff-
face of fire and flood.

Over there, Raymond, that's still the old gentleman, casting light
on his face with a match from illuminating his cigar a short moment ago and looking you in the face now, his mouth open, out of

which the cigar dropped to the ground just a second ago; it's lying at his feet like a stranded firefly now, and the question arises
as to why he didn't smoke it to the end, why his open mouth is
now emitting a despairing lament, a question that in fact makes
it binding on you to give a clear answer: "Why did you shoot
me?"

And you're all ready to give him an answer in words upspoken—
"I didn't shoot you": so as if to prove your answer you turn your
face downward, toward the ground, whereupon there comes into
your view, in your own hand, taking you completely by surprise
but pointing right at your hands as if to verify the deed—to your
complete amazement you see your pistol, although that doesn't
have to mean you fired it, not by a long shot, and why smoke is
coming out of the barrel can be explained by the evening mist of
this autumn day having seeped into the weapon earlier and, as
anyone can plainly see, now oozing back out as a small trail of
mist, not smoke.
Meanwhile the old man has collapsed and is lying at your feet; he
must have been shot from behind by somebody who was in fact
aiming at you, intending to hit you; don't you somehow feel you
really must have been hit, or is it the pain of the old man, whose
injury from a wound-inflicting projectile is causing him ferocious
waves of agony now transmitted from him to you, meaning that
what you have been designated to do for him is to relieve his pain
by taking it on yourself, or something like that.
Finally Captain Murray ahead of him Matell and his wife cursing
them out gun pointed at them about to be booked for black-
market dealings under arrest ordering them to get into the jeep
and be quick about it and now bawling you out why weren't you
sitting in the jeep all this time we have to disappear as fast as we
can this whole situation is turning out all wrong but we can sal-
vage it anyway all right we didn't earn a red cent tonight but still
we're in luck this mess is a trap we've turned back on them

Tell me, Raymond, gunning down this truly important composer
just like that?!
Tell me, couldn't that somehow or other have been avoided?
Tell me, was it you who fired or was it, as you're stating, somebody else who fired?

Tell me: you once and he twice or he once and you only twice?
You really don't know anything?
Yes, it's a crying shame about drinkers, and when their memory
oozes away, there's nothing that can be done. You were blinded—
dazzled all of a sudden, as you say. Then everything at such
lightning speed in the rapid flash that it then struck your eyesight
deaf.
You're asking—but you can't seriously mean it—why John, the
driver, couldn't just as well have been the one to open fire, because he was outside as well, just like you. You can't seriously
mean that. And which John do you mean anyway?
Tell me, isn't it possible that no driver came along with you that
evening, because Captain Murray wanted to drive the jeep himself, since he was very suspicious that evening and didn't want
any witnesses? So which John, then? Is there any such person at
all? Nobody knows anything about him; he's just not there.
Wasn't there. Will not be able to have been there at all, at any
time. Must be confusing him with someone else.

Do you know, Raymond, who the man is you shot? His name is
Dr. Anton Webern. Doesn't mean a thing to you. Born back in the
last century in Vienna. But you don't care anything about that either. I'll tell you about him anyway—his father was a high rank-
ing official in the old Royal and Imperial Austro-Hungarian gov-
ernment, posted to a duchy in the south, to a city named Klagenfurt, that is, where Tony had to attend the liberal-arts prepara-
tory school, soon learned to play the cello, soon started writing
his first songs and small pieces for various and sundry instruments, until one day he was finally able to move back to Vienna,
where he occupied several rooms at the university dedicated to
musicology, but then—and this is beyond a doubt the most cru-
cial, the most appropriate decision he would ever, in his whole
life, make on his own behalf—went to whatever lengths it took to
become a pupil of Arnold Schönberg, which he succeeded in doing, as a result learning from him all about how to compose au-
thentically, how to create sounds never before heard by any ear
and to make them audible for the first time, albeit almost all of
his first pieces were more or less jeered at and booed, or at best
ignored with the keenest of interest, and then too the poor man
had to conduct operetta all over Europe, because he was forced

to earn a lot of money for his wife and daughter, then his second daughter and then his son as well, though he couldn't stand it in any one place for very long, which is why he drifted all throughout Europe, forced over and over again to move from one city to another, because, to look at it from the opposite point of view, no city could stand him after a while either, no city was about to put up with his battling the operetta repertory and mercilessly berating the singers as clothes-horse tenors. Until sheer misery made him sick in Stettin and he couldn't move a single step after the fire curtain, somehow torn loose, almost severed his head from his body, bending as he was taking a bow after a premiere, the man almost guillotined as his body was bowing to an audience busy booing him and ready to rip his head off themselves after the fire curtain went wide of its aim; fortunately only his glasses lay shattered on the stage, all the world being a stage, remember, though not to him, for whom the stage was no part of any world at all, much though it might be to everybody else, because they never let any other kind of world except the one right in front of them enter their heads.

Everything's proceeding very smoothly, Ray, and you have nothing to fear, because they're not going to file charges against you, as you just heard the judge, the major, say, since you were credible in presenting to the court that you believed you were acting in self-defense, that fire flaring up with lightning-quick silence! Felt threatened by the sudden lifting of a match to the cigar and never attempted, not even by so much as a hint, to testify that in your opinion you couldn't have shot anyone, since the whole world seems to be firm in maintaining that no one other than you could have killed the composer, who has only now, posthumously, been cleared of any suspicion of having taken part in black-market dealings, and, for that matter, the judge is offering condolences to everyone involved for suffering incurred, especially, of course, to the widow of the deceased composer, who had previously explained how and why she and her husband had been invited for the evening to this house, belonging to their daughter and son-in-law, and then how her husband had been so hoping for his first cigar in a long time, how he had been looking forward to it like a child, and then, as the grandchildren were being put to bed in their room, Doctor Webern, whom the cigar wouldn't let rest

easy, and who had in mind to smoke it outside, at the front of the
house, not wanting smoke to drift through the rooms, having in
mind that it might bother the children, stepped out into the
doorway.

And you, Raymond, fourteen days' confinement to quarters as a
protection against yourself and the public at large till it's time for
them to send you home.

Raymond, do you still mean anything to yourself? Or have you
really fallen so far away from yourself that you no longer even
hope to find yourself, not even far past that point your eyes can
still reach as they look out the window? Oblivious then, forgetting all about yourself, you still haven't forgotten that you
learned cooking as a trade, after which you traveled all over,
hither and yon, from the roaring ovens of Alaska to the deep-
freeze lockers of Hawaii, finally one day winding up in that small
town along the beach on the Atlantic coast in North Carolina,
where you almost became head chef at that huge hotel there, if
only that three-star accommodation hadn't degenerated not long
afterwards into a whore house for the military, you nonetheless
very happy just to stay right there where you were, if only the war
hadn't brought you over here, transported you to this place, to
this village amid the Alps, the name of which even its inhabitants
are happy to forget, and where, right up to now, preventive
measures—the day-in-and-day-out, lethargically puking, rebel-
lious field kitchens of the *Rainbow Division*—have to be taken
over and over again to thwart the constant wish to go AWOL.

Locked up, you say? Not at all; it's just that you can no longer
open this door quite so easily, quite so naturally, as you used to;
it's a little stiff. Look, though, look over there; don't you see him,
isn't that perhaps how it was? Doctor Webern was—exactly like
just now—was himself the door you couldn't get through and
can't get through now either, or might it be even more likely that
you were the door in the bending slipstream of which, bent over,
he put a match to his cigar?

Two doors facing each other—two entryways, each facing the
other and each wanting to open the other—two doors desiring to
pass by way of their door sashes one through the other and into
each other, each of them in turn opened out, double door by
double door, each having passed through the other's sash with

just about room to spare them double-doorpanel backandforth
face-slapping when they're done, hard to believe each has passed
through the other, that's what they mean to each other, these
door sashes, neither uprooting the other, but then on the way
back slamming the door hard on each other, now this loud bang,
now having to fling their doors back open at each other, hard,
these two sashes or entryways, as if they had just now lost the
capacity to avoid clashing, each rearing back, hauling off, opening its door out wide to slam it hard again, like a horse rearing
back for a hard kick, two mounts, hooves thrust upward through
the air at a slant, slamming hard rearward, each into the other,
and the two panels of the double doors in the gateways now torn
out of their hinges, ending up wide open on top of each other,
smashing each other to pieces in the dust, their door frames
empty, each fleeing from the other as they rush off in opposite
directions, each in its own way breathlessly sashed and clashed
and smashed, out toward the horizon, to shatter in utter exhaustion at the enclosing wall along the edge of the panorama.

And you—what an unforgettable hero! Where are your letters;
don't you keep a diary; not a single scrap in the drawer; no note
book, no address book—couldn't you at least have a small map of
the country on you, or something like armed forces' post cards
you're thinking of sending; don't you write to anybody, ever? Not
even to your wife? Isn't there anything that points to you?

No? Oh all right, at least a little pistol for you to fire. That's
something, anyway. Not much, though. In fact, it's less than
nothing. You stole it, after all, so it doesn't belong to you; rather,
it's a relative of the war, which you never wanted to get into but
now don't really want to get out of.

Tell me, Raymond, who back over there in Europe do you think
is now supposed to conduct those gigantic symphonies of Gustav
Mahler and again make them resound as only Doctor Webern
was able to? You have to understand, Ray, that these are symphonies as large as the sea, ones that Doctor Webern, before the
war, casting his fierce gaze into the waves of the North Sea or the
Baltic Sea, used to conduct by standing on the shore and dictat-
ing the volume of the storm clouds, though mainly having to turn
directly to the surging breakers, until he brought them to the
point that their pounding flood-tide spume and spray subordi-

nated themselves with great willingness to the authority of his baton.

You most likely don't believe that. But just take a look out there, look farther away, over the country, along the train tracks, out through the evening, look over there; his widow has just now arrived back in Vienna and is at her house, severely damaged by the war. Look how she's reaching under charred beams and pulling things out of the ruins of her former life, small things, so tiny they can't even be seen from here, and now someone else is with her, probably a neighbor, by whom Frau Webern is no sooner welcomed back than she's being offered condolences, but with such loud lamentations you can almost hear them from here—she just couldn't believe it, she heard it from her daughter-in-law and just didn't want to believe it, at the very last, when it was all over, Americans, too, well they're usually not like that, are they, supposedly Doctor Webern was standing on a balcony down there in Mittersill, giving some kind of speech, wasn't he, and then when he raised his his right arm at the end, they misunderstood, right?

By way of answer the widow can do nothing more than shake her head and go on shaking her head, interrupted by various and sundry kinds of questions, but then this neighbor woman takes her down into the cellar, where there awaits her a high mountain of newspapers, letters, papers of all kinds, which she then starts making a hopeless attempt to sort, crying, of course—what else would she be doing—while the neighbor is comforting her in an effort to stop her crying; she wants to help, which she does by saying more or less that if she'd had any idea her neighbors the Weberns would ever come back she would have straightened the place up as much as she could, but as you can imagine, almost everything went up in smoke anyway, Frau Webern, all of it was personal property, too, wasn't it, nobody else's business and certainly not these Red agents of the Russians, who snooped through everything, keeping a close lookout for spying and suspecting it everywhere, not long ago, for example, going all through the neighborhood and copying whatever names they pleased out of people's personal correspondence, immediately after which the building superintendent from the house across the street was shipped off to Siberia within a matter of hours, and so on and so on.

At last Frau Webern is alone; you can see her by candlelight there in the cellar, glancing through old letters, sheets of music, postcards; she's becoming calmer all the time, almost serene; you can see her face remembering, and this remembering is growing ever brighter and happier for her. Look how she's making her way ever closer to her husband, Doctor Webern, deeper and deeper, back to the beginning of their time together, closer to his memory in the present, amid this paper heap of surging breakers destroyed by fire and flood—washed into the cellar, deluged back to earth—reading letters about how they got through their long separations by staying attuned to each other like two instruments each tuning to the other, Danzig, beach along the sea, talking as they walked, words into sentences whose beachword responses, leaning toward each other shorelong, moving shorealong, tuning harmoniously, questions of wordmaking back and forth asway, two instrumental melodies shorealong bending each other aright to rights, each soaring deeper and dropping higher with the other, wandering dunes fluting sandhigh inward to land, overtaut strings slackened in the orchestra pit of the beach finding each other now after all in talking while walking, as all the while she confuses things, her memory, now transferred from remembering into actually experiencing, so that memory has become actual experience for her, is carrying her now right through the walk they took back in those days, Danzig, beach along the sea, now become real the talks from that time, now being then, and if she has now, in person, and together with him, gone from back there, from that time to this place, thus hither from thither, remembering in a round her way to here, has remembered her way back to experience, once and for all making her way back from there, as it was easier to do then; they would have soared upward like the two wings of a bird, swelling over the world and yet farther, lightupward, inward an auditorium of air for presenting a rainbow, which would be on the stage—the performance having just begun—leaning against a podium of clouds to hold its gleaming speech of colors, all scattered far and wide across the land. And the widow of the composer, by doing less and less remembering and more and more experiencing of her late—but by now not so late—husband through her return to Vienna, to the war-torn house, by now really experiencing her memories instead of remembering her experiences, having earlier watched and listened, together with her husband, to the color speech of the rainbow, and by having now a living experience of her memory of being swept up, together with her husband, in the content of that same rainbow's color speech, and via her memory, a living experience as now transmuted into an experience they were still able to live through together, is flung in the flight of the rainbow backward from its colors to Vienna, into a time shortly before the end of the living experiences they went through together, each with the other, into this very house whose cellar Frau Webern is leaving as she now climbs the stairs to one of the rooms, the study, behind the closed doors of which Doctor Webern, alone, deserted by almost the whole world, has buried himself for the duration and shut himself off from his oblivion, a state into which the entire rest of the world has plunged him and which, until almost the end of the war, he refused to allow to come flooding over him, just as a desert plant buried in the sand, forgetful of itself in the arid season, can only send out shoots and again swim lightupward with the onset of a rain whose coming has long seemed unlikely—this was the kind of perseverance Doctor Webern exercised in waiting throughout the entire war for his son to come home, and until that time the closed doors of his study would withstand the massive gushing torrents of being swept by oblivion out of the world, until the time was right for him to be awash in the flood waters, at least until now, when his wife went up to the second floor of the house, through the doors of that same study, and walked right up to him without alerting him in advance by knocking, stood before him almost frozen by a message sufficient to make him almost freeze as well, the content of which at first almost causes the sunbeams themselves to fall victim to total paralysis and subjects the room to a spaceclearing lightwhirling engorgement outward from the room, out of the window, to the light in the room as the eye of a typhoon in the utter collapse of his study, which has just about gone flowing through the keyhole, while he hears words coming from his wife: Peter . . . war . . . will not be returning home . . . fell . . . fallen . . . dead . . . burial cannot take place here . . . already buried . . . in the midst of war . . . whereupon, after a very short period of their both standing there fossilized, with the air of the room wafting around them, each suddenly realized the pointlessness of persevering any further and made a sudden decision, without having to say anything to each other, to seek refuge from the war by heading west, quite as if, after waking from their paralysis, they had planned between them never again, if at all possible, to allow themselves to be frozen out of time for whatever time remained to them during the rest of their lives and, furthermore, not to force upon themselves in even the slightest degree the obligation of observing with their own eyes the destruction of Vienna—meaning, to him, at any rate, the musical center of the entire world even still—neither by the approaching troops of the Red Army nor by any other insanely world-subjugating vortexby-landproducing, military gearandmeshdriven, detonating explosivedevicesoutfitted fanatics, each refusing any longer to stand by as the other endures lightblasting woundproducing fury arising out of the command authority of any and all timeincinerating earthstaggering worldigniting masters, in addition to there by now being too much gone lost to their eyes by way of a former future, drapes drawn back too soon, plunging to the floor, as waterfalls plunge down mountainsides and cut off the surrounding view from valleys that slope downward from the sky.

Do you see, Raymond? Take a look at how they've already got everything packed up, taking along only what's really important, fleeing the house, away from the house, on foot. Doctor Webern comes back once more, though, before you can again return to your foreign place there on the other side of the Atlantic Ocean, to cross which by ship you boarded the next train heading away from the valley and thought by taking a seat in it you would leave this war behind forever, tossing it behind your back out the train window like some odds and ends left in your memory, which seems no longer to have been able to succeed very well in making out of your return a never-ending homecoming but only in bringing you resolution in fragments, bits and pieces.

How very often they have tried, how very often, to drive him, Doctor Webern, out of Vienna, the city in which he has not indeed been really present for a long time anyway, and now he is finally going away from there to return to this valley forever, and if the Russians weren't coming, he would have stayed, would still be there, buried in Vienna with snubbing kindnesses, friendly slanders, thoughtfulness of the most boorish sort, courtesy at its most insolent, buried alive amidst a welter of intrigues by the Viennese, who nonetheless learn, albeit not until much later, how to earn a tidy sum out of every one of the ever more frequent and advantageous business arrangements for sold-out concerts featuring the world-renewing sound creations he has left behind.

Away from the world capital of music, as people are fond of seeing this city, although what they almost always mean is the so-called Viennese waltz, which is Metternich music! Or—in possession of a rickety music stand that once belonged to Mozart, having as their very own Schubert's spittoon (a cup for their herbal tea) and his chamber pot (their salad bowl), both fashioned with loving care out of highly valuable Augarten porcelain hand-trimmed with painted floral decorations around the edges—they fancy themselves musical; or else they keep on dragging out the junk they have hidden away in a broom closet, persistent, innocent, mendacious little narratives, lies dangerous in general, with all the defamatory pride of anecdotes recounted with a flourish, the stories constantly retold, rumors really, about the *Dreimäderlhaus*, the place where Schubert supposedly had lodgings with three simpering young women, the tales all enveloped in a frowzy cloud cover of stale air from shared toilets along the corridor, the length and breadth of the hallway featuring rehashings of musical stories which the bombs will now annihilate, at least if wishes really do come true! In any actual music itself the Viennese have much less interest than in the rumors that lie on every side, and if the same pieces, ones conducive to the operational smoothness of their alimentary processes, are not played all the time in their concerts, then these subscribers, ensconced in their seats forever, hold their ears, at least insofar as they are not sitting on them, in cases where the latter have grown out of their posteriors and not their heads, only too eager to revile as atonal feces in sound, as cacophony, what they have not even heard, and if they could, to file police charges for public disturbance of the peace, but now these eardrum syphilitics are for once getting to hear what genuine cacophony in fact is; it's of course and at best the atonality of Stalin's organs—so now he is at last really leaving Vienna, having had by now not only his fill of accusations, his fill of being taxed with treasonous disrespect by a conglomeration of dried-up music-stand scarecrows in all their decayed piety, but to top it all off—as if it weren't enough that so many had banished him, had barred entry through the doors of everyone's ears to his music, had pasted onto him the label of *"entartet"* or "degenerate" composer and defamed his creations, the very essence of sound, as acoustically monstrous, deformed things posing a threat to the people of the German master race and their one-station radio receivers—beyond all that, quite a number of them now turn coat at the very last minute and are prepared to heap him with insult by declaring that he snatched at the main chance, climbed the ladder by turning diehard Nazi, only because he loved a few poems by Hölderlin and made known which ones, it so happening that they were the identical ones that supposedly occasioned just such pleasure and approbation on the part of the German *Führer*. It's the icing on the cake that suddenly Doctor Webern is supposed to have become a Nazi. But now he has truly returned home, to those other mountains, whose tops, enclosing this forgotten valley of the peace prevailing in the region lying at their feet, represent the stone fortifications placed by their appointed superiors to maintain surveillance over the coming times of bogus peace in this postwar period just begun, Raymond, and its deeply obscured heritage of your own status as a survivor, as one left remaining, a status on which you turn your back in this railroad train now leaving the valley, while, looking out through the window, you are unwilling to catch even a glimpse of anything in your memory, and now, while your face in the train window suddenly gets a glimpse of itself floating back into the coach, you get a sudden glance—yes, you do; don't get scared; it's once again so direct all of a sudden—look, take a close look at him, look right square into the middle of his face, yes, it's really him, it's Doctor Webern, you know it is, and can you hear, can't you hear yourself, in a great fright, saluting him cordially without words, what a delightful surprise to see you again, Doctor Webern, what a wonderful twist of fate to be face to face with each other once more, just at this point in our life, and speaking of points, there's one particular point which perhaps for the time being at least we really needn't talk about, not yet anyway, because mentioning it would be likely to have an unpleasant effect on us, since after all this pain-inducing state of being torn away from each other, to the point of being torn apart, being torn away until just now could well have—

Totally unexpectedly and without wasting a word he, this man whom you allegedly shot, replies to your wordless, lost isolation out of an altogether grateful isolation of his own, to thank you, this man allegedly shot by you saying that in fact he has you to thank, not for saving his life in any way, of course, but—through the supposed use of the weapon, which after all you might well have actually been brave enough to aim at him, Ray—for having been the cause of his, the composer's, at last being able to breathe, to heave a sigh of relief, to feel, as it were, an entire mountain range drop from his heart and go tumbling down, by which he has in mind that boring chain of the Felber Tauern mountains back behind where he is living, and he is in fact explaining to you that only after you and everything about your person appeared on the scene had it become possible for him to bring to a conclusion the complete acoustical oeuvre, in the perfection of its final form, of the person he was, which has made him very happy, "whether you're now able in any degree to believe me or not, young man, and any questions about whys and wherefores have confronted you with nothing but riddles the solutions to which have yet to yield you any meaning or explanation, because in the end it is in this one single tone, within the silence of whose secluded nature and connected with whose undertones and overtones all other tones whatever were invited to resonate as well—yes, it is in this one tone, as indeed in every other tone whatever as well that in the end the history of the entire world was contained, all the way from the cataclysm at the beginning to the constancy of isolation at the ultimate ending; and as far as you are concerned, too, that is quite enough of inexplicability for your person, an answer adequate to the unanswerably riddling or puzzling quality of your own shape, merely a last-ditch, very specific musical or at least sound-producing instrument, just as the very specific musical instrument you held in your hand at that time is to be handled with the greatest of skill, as indeed, during the course of your much too brief concert, you enjoyed the great success of producing with absolute accuracy and at the precise pitch and volume stipulated in the score the final three notes you played during the last piece—with your threefold shots and the loud reports, the explosive banging sounds directed at my person, you enabled me, through none other than those bang, bang, bang sounds, to draw to a conclusion most

credible to all the world, made it possible for me simply to bring
to an end, signaling its closure by way of a musically perfect culminating chord, the finale of my life, a life made up of musical
sounds; but there's something I wanted to ask you, too—is there
by any chance a lever or capo mounted somewhere on your musical instrument that would allow your device to transpose, if you
wanted it to, the report from each separate shot—just as an example—yet deeper into the bass range or into the sound quality
of a coloratura scream; that would be such a great improvement,
so where would a lever like that be; could you just show it to
me?"

You know this gentleman sitting opposite you, don't you, Doctor
Webern? You don't? Then I definitely must set about introducing
you to each other. This is Mr. Raymond Norwood Bell, presently
on his way home; he just now looked you straight in the face; he
thought you were somehow trying to cut across his shady dealings—what an unfortunate mutual misunderstanding; it put a
black mark on everything—but he did after all just now apparently compose for your work those three first-rate tones that just
couldn't make their way out of your pen—too bad he has to leave
so soon; why does he have to rush away so quickly, hurrying
along the corridor of the coach to get outside—he still has exactly
one decade, after all, to set his hand to the door at the end of the
corridor, trying his hand at an everlasting return home, finally by
himself on the farther side of the Atlantic, arrivalhood-
struggling, though in vain, on his home continent, lasting only a
fleeting moment, arriving for so very short a span and then
caught in surroundings having no reality for him, in a memory
whose continuity into the present has been broken off with no
prospect of a future, very likely unable, in this oblivion to self,
ever to happen upon any point of his true arrival that would not
at once be lost to his sight before drowned glances grasp him.
Too bad; even as very brief as it is, even the fleeting moment of
his coming back to the small spot in the middle of South Carolina
that he calls home is no more than an illusion—his happiness at
just having arrived, trying to make his erratically swaying body
get up and leave the bus, his immediately seeing that he is face to
face and almost in collision with the first sight of his wife, into
whose path he steps, as if she had caught him at something, see-

ing her body as it starts to board the bus from which he has just emerged and glancing at her and, frightened and overjoyed at one and the same time, calling out to her, "The war is over . . . I'm back!" And she, while her body disappears inside the bus, answers him and calls back, "In a hurry . . . school at nine . . . food in the refrigerator . . . please try not to drink till tonight, when I'm back . . . stay sober . . . at least until then!"

What's the matter with her, Doctor Webern? What's wrong with his wife? What has happened in her life? Probably he never wrote her back throughout all the long years of the war, to which he lost her, not welcomed back *by* her because he never said goodbye *to* her and thus, with no farewell, has remained behind, invisibly never absent by being ever present (if not accounted for), lacking any actual presence of an absence, now evaporated from her sight—and there he is, remaining behind, left alone by the departing bus, imagining that he has arrived home; his body is there to see, of course, but anyone reaching a hand out to him would just be grasping the empty air, because even as far as he himself is concerned he has already disappeared from where he seems to be, and what there still is to be seen of the silhouette belonging to this man who one might suppose has returned to his home over there is merely a hollow mirroring of his figure in thin air, hurled away from this valley and across the Atlantic Ocean, there to dwell under a sky that no longer, not even once, showers down on him the cheapest of booze, as in France the absinthe dripped right out of the clouds and straight into his mouth or in Austria torrential waterfalls of delectable beer gushed with all the freshness of a new spring from breweries atop Alpine peaks and inundated him in the most mouth-watering way; yes, this man is a heavy drinker, unfortunately, and there's nothing more that can be done, just as every real drinker has to be looked upon as a drowning man, one whom the drink is pulling down into the drink, one who flails about and fights off every rescuer swimming toward him, in his turn pushing the rescuer under water before it's even possible to hold a lifesaving hand out to him.

A heavy drinker: yes, Raymond, you heard correctly, but that's not a reprimand; on the contrary, it's actually—though it has gone behind your back to coil itself all around your person, as it were—a commendation, a tribute of the highest order, in fact! Because if all soldiers were to start drinking like maniacs before wars broke out, no one would ever be able to fight any war; instead, opposing batallions would have no choice but to collapse into each other's arms at drying-out hospitals, the men driven through the doors of those institutions by their wives and girlfriends—that means you, too, Raymond, because wasn't your wife trying even before the war to get you admitted to a treatment center for withdrawal, not to say attempting over and over to get you locked up for life in an insane asylum, shutting you away from the world forever if she could, though you were naturally still in a position to prevent from happening everything she wanted to do to you, things you didn't want to have done to you, that is, even if there was just no doing anything with you any more—well, it's true, isn't it—but at least not that, not yet, and you were able to escape it all by going to war, able to elude all those angels out to save you, women who, as prison guards and wardens of well-meaningness, their commitment being to your commitment, were tempted in their mean-spiritedness to lock you away, just like Doctor Webern in the prisons of his operettas—and it turned out that he likewise understood how to defend himself with great strength by constantly being able to escape over and over again their martialmusicchord prison guards, their mush rendering all real sounds defenseless.

You need to make money, Doctor Webern, I'm sure, so it's off to your operetta, meaning long separations from your own music, colloquies with yourself as you walk along the beach by the sea in Danzig, loosening those overtaut strings, and then you find you're in Stettin, along the beach once more, by the sea, until the exact right tuning is finally achieved; you've got to get to a rehearsal, where are you, you're late, where have you been, oh I see, that's where, Doctor Webern, as always in the beginning, over and over again until the very last, that is, stuck at some nearby point (right in front of you, amid barren theatrical wastelands that evoke fear-tinged laughter) of workaday devastation by operetta; once again the first sighting of the sea, which causes alarm each time all over again, because even the most penetrating glance can neither bore deeper past nor glide away beyond the surface of the water, the eyes losing themselves instead in what they cannot glimpse while the drowning glance runs out of air. For the municipal operetta theater forced on you here, however, there's no finding any expression. People go to see operetta so they can have served up to them—masquerading on stage as nice, kind actions—all the petty, mean-spirited deeds they engage in outside of operetta, and they keep going back until such time as the snide and sneaky ways they pursue outside of operetta are ready, willing, and able, because of the sugar-coating operetta applies to them, to seem sweet and nice, as a result of which people can experience their whole existence as one big operetta, since now any mean-spirited act can be construed as some terrifically sweet and nice deed, in that way smoothing things out by making the workaday gray-out of feeling closely akin to and an integral part of every life that's lovable. As you set out on the walk you are about to take along the beach you would naturally much rather go on conducting the symphony orchestra of the sea, those light-drenched fanfarechord chorales breaking forth just up ahead, soaring upward into the air; clear away all that crap, you are so right, it would be doing the world a favor to herd every operetta ever written out past the pounding surf and into the deep blue sea, to round them all up and with great circumspection to conduct each and every last one of them out beyond the horizon, off and away to the other side, so far off that not a single operetta would ever again be able to break over your brow, to crash over your head: get to rehearsal; you have a rehearsal at four, and today's the last day you're going to let that clothes-horse tenor get away with it; you're going to warn him for the last time and threaten to interrupt the performance at this point—including at the premiere itself, if need be—should he yet again sing the passage sloppily, because even music that arouses the deepest loathing has to be intoned accurately and cleanly, and even when the music is telling lies, the notes have to be played in such a way that the melodies inscribed in the operetta scores, pathological liars though they may be, have to be intoned and executed less to arouse bliss than to be rendered correctly and strictly within the prescribed time signature, so that the true character of the false musicianship in these works can be made evident instead of being distorted.

How to even start escaping a theater like this and the need to deal with people like these (or any other people, for that matter), because through your forced contacts with such people you can't stand another second of anything, not anything at all, in your current position as *the* head of operetta, responsible for functioning as the smooth operettor, if not operator—on days like today, days that clamp themselves around your body like everchanging, workaday cities all looking alike and, along with all their buildings gathered together and tied around you as well, choking off everything else by the huddled slums of the architectural designs of your operetta stages, in considering which you, hounded from one city to another, see yourself as being constantly in need of moving on, finding new quarters.

Operetta: what homage to divine migraine and its elevation to supercelestial sclerosis amidst angels and archangels, onward and upward, unto the state of attaining eternal salvation amidst the irreversibly supervening heavenly hardening of the Holy Spirit's arteries!
Operetta: Ascension into Heaven of Holy Malaria! Beatified Polio, Supernal Typhoid Fever, Ambrosian Cholera, Hoof and Mouth Disease in the Garden of Eden!
You have to apply from the beginning all over again every time, in all German-speaking cities, Doctor Webern, but unfortunately it's unbearable no matter where you are; but what about this, Doctor Webern: wouldn't it be simpler to go about it in reverse for once? Suppose, instead of moving to a different city, as you've always done before, you were just to remain in place when you've once more (as is now the case yet again) been driven beyond endurance—suppose you chased the present city away and then waited for other cities to come flying through the sky for the purpose of making application to you, managers and artistic directors having to inquire of you from above (rather than your inquiring of them) whether you might find it agreeable to have them drop the theater in question down from the sky and onto your head.

Yet another winter without composing, and when you don't compose you don't exist.
So you send this city packing; clear away all that crap indeed, which process you initiate by chasing this city away; you won't let it go on bringing you down, so you simply order the municipal administration building, along with all the other buildings, being

more or less adept at soaring overland, to lift off from the ground
and in a twinkling—with every single building in this city tucked
up and folded in, fluttering roofwingupward in wild hutswarms
through the prolonged rotting of an atmospheric space filled with
dense roomflocks of dwellings drifting off course—to vanish and
to take up residence at some other operetta spot somewhere else
in this world; so here we are, Doctor Webern, and you're now
waiting until (it's over your head) new and unknown cities come
flying this way over your head and come in for a landing, their
cables, made of stringnetstreets and neighborhoodavenueinter-
twinings, tugged all taut around the houses fastened to them and
around the applause of those residing in them (an applause entirely appropriate to the moment and being sounded with people's hands over their heads), by means of which occurrences
your family first and foremost, Doctor Webern, will now at last,
once and for all, be spared the former stresses and strains of all
those moves and those relocations, inasmuch as you will finally
remain where you are and the various and sundry cities come flying past one by one, hover above you in the sky, and call down a
question as to whether or not—all depending—you might or
might not find it agreeable to authorize buildings, squares, and
boulevardravinestreetblocks, in that order, along with all the foo-
thills of neighborhoods and suburbs, to come drifting downward
and, upon conferral of the permission to land previously requested by them of your esteemed self, to drop right down on
your head as fast as possible, leaving aloft neither kit nor caboo-
dle, while in the midst of hastily trying to press for appointments
with you and setting in motion all appropriate theatrical hue and
cry—
or better yet, you will have several cities all range themselves
around you at the same time, have them gathered around you
until such time as almost all the cities of this continent, spanned
around and about you and your esteemed person, Doctor Webern, have made their way to you, all their houses and buildings
lying in close proximity to your operetta landscape, Doctor Webern, extending in far-reaching operettisization across the ter-
rain of your musical activities and around your person, not ex-
cluding such remaining cities as have never yet gone on a journey, setting forth after overcoming the most weighty of obstacles,
great town mansions fuddled in mortar, walled up and in, folded

up and in and bridging the air in the course of a wall-fluttering
trip through the wide atmosphere, roof-winged giants all, and also those flocks of birds, almost mythically forgotten by now, of
the one-eyed ocean giants all vying to drown one another in the
Atlantic for the prize of a blue ribbon; yes, indeed, Doctor Webern, clear away all that crap, until one day all are at last duly
and properly—thanks to your highly valued leadership with responsibility as the smooth operettor—placed under your highly
respected charge for the purpose of producing in exactly the
same way exactly the same continually performed, all-
encompassing, single, solitary cosmic operetta, one that contains
all other operettas within itself, tossed off with panache under
your judicious leadership, thereby breaching a gradually apprehensible state of world encirclement, world-disappearingly connected in its turn to a single, solitary, though indubitably extant
globe-encircling operetta tastelessness, caused by you—along
with its tacky trade in religious objects (wholesale)—to come
tumbling down through established proof-lie-entruthment, to
tear away from its moorings, to sink into some trap-door stage-
rigged undercroft, to achieve a gradual finality in the process of
sinking ever deeper before the eyes of the whole audience, undergoing burial by a consensus that takes on binding force, and,
as for the rest, for the first time finally attaining the permanently
valid conclusiveness of a most irretrievable, most impressive oblivion, Doctor Webern, sent hurtling out beyond the horizon,
Doctor Webern; clear away all that crap—wouldn't it be quite
something, Doctor Webern, to sweep away all this heavenly inan-
ity by just lifting your little finger?
Which is all well and good, Doctor Webern, but first you have urgent business in Prague. Don't tell me you forgot! Don't you understand? You don't understand, do you—why Prague, why now?
As you see it—in your view, that is, now, if at all—well, at least
Vienna beforehand, not Prague, not yet, first Vienna; but no,
there's no beforehand, not even Vienna; in your view you could
squeeze in some other place, if anything at all, maybe Plauen,
Breslau, Cracow, but no, and not Bad Ischl either, Doctor Webern, that was back at the beginning, that's all over and done
with, I'm sure you don't want to squeeze in a place like Marburg
on the Drau first—and did you in fact mean Marburg on the
Drau, so easily confused with Marburg on the Lahn (which is

even better than the town on the Drau)—because Klagenfurt has just rejected you again, has passed you by once more, which means a quick trip to Graz; if only you hadn't now and then been so eager in your desire to go to Prague, where better conditions, owing to General Music Director Zemlinsky, are awaiting you, albeit awkward hindrances unfortunately keep forestalling a final arrangement, so that this one hope for an acceptable way of earning your bread as a musician is fraught with circumstances which, though they don't strike you as set up exclusively for the purpose of killing you off, nonetheless cause one postponement after another, threatening to sweep this prospect out past your field of vision; so then first to Osnabrück—that's right, isn't it, Doctor Webern?—and then Danzig again, and then, worst of all, unfortunately, then Stettin, where not long ago the fire curtain almost severed your head from your shoulders as you were taking a bow—and reluctantly, at that, forced into it—after a premiere, something or somebody or it itself acting on its own ("it" being the curtain), quite as efficiently as if deliberate aim had been taken, the curtain plummeting downward like a guillotine toward your neck, toward the shoulders of your inclined figure such that it would have chopped your head right off just as you had finished abashedly lowering your eyes to avoid meeting the gaze of a booing audience, the fortunate upshot of the mishap, however, being that only your glasses were smashed; you're right, Doctor Webern, about not going to Prague right away, your first urgent need now was to squeeze in Vienna after all, the city where operetta launched a massive counterattack and nearly scored a full hit, landed a knockout blow in the war you started against it; yes, it's urgently necessary for your recovery that you squeeze Vienna in—Vienna, yes, finally Vienna once again, and then, that long-yearned-for offer from Prague should only now come at last, Zemlinsky doing his best to hire you because Schönberg has convinced him through exhaustive detail how absolutely essential you and your musical qualities are to him, the general music director in Prague, extending you an offer of a position in Prague, especially well remunerated at one hundred crowns, personally taking special pains to obtain your services, it being granted to you at last that you can settle in Prague, temporarily, to be sure, but also for some considerable time, an offer that allows you and your family, especially in comparison with

conditions earlier, a transitional period of pause and recupera-
tion, with everything you need being set straight down in your
path. Still, you once again composed nothing throughout this
whole past winter, Doctor Webern, and remember: when you
don't compose you don't even exist; at least that's what you always say about yourself, and quite rightly, too, and so you might
cautiously pose a question to yourself, only very slightly ques-
tionable though it may be, but perhaps with some curiosity on
your own part as to the answer or even the reason for asking—tell
me, Doctor Webern (as you ask yourself), do you still in fact exist, or do you first have to compose at least a little something in
order to exist really and truly, at least halfway?
However that may be, you still have an urgent need to go to Prague, Doctor Webern; better get a move on, you have no time to
lose, matters are pressing, so don't just stand there—get going!
Don't tell me you're staying stuck where you are, stuck hidden
away on that little street in Vienna where your path is now
blocked, piled sky high with furniture from a vacated apartment—oh, but you're stepping up now and even adding to the
pile by lumbering over to it with more furniture, teaming up with
one of the moving men to carry an old bedframe through the
house door, over the sidewalk, across the paved surface of the
street and into that huge vehicle, a furniture-moving van that has
all of a sudden pulled up and into the dark cavern of which every
stick of the furnishings from your apartment has in short order
done a vanishing act, the van completely loaded up and ready to
drive off, its crew having already boarded it in the natural course
of events, the engine started and the vehicle set in motion, slowly, briefly, deceleration-sputtering while making its way gingerly
along the street as you call out by way of a goodbye greeting into
the rolled-down window on the driver's side of the cab, the driver's profile standing out like a black-seared silhouette against the
opposing light, a few of the more pertinent among the following
words and phrases applicable to the situation, words like strips
of material for making banners, like shreds torn from tarpaulin
coverings, erratically flapping in the morning light, small sha-
dow-remnants of a flame died away, gliding away all murk-
burned frayed, mistcharring broken bits of sentences coming out
of your mouth, Doctor Webern, even as you are flinging toward
the driver's face, turned back to meet yours, and causing to land

smack dab on his head the following rags and tags of words: "Off
to Prague, then; away you go; oh, but do you have the slip of paper with the exact address?; no, that's not the right paper; you
should have it on you, or have you lost it?; no, show it to me anyway, please just show me the right little scrap so I can set my
mind at rest"—followed, as a goodbye greeting, by a waving motion (though you can't even begin to make out what it is) from a
handkerchief fully aflutter in the headwind, final flurryfluttering
farewell flung to your figure, sad, left behind there, stuck to the
pavement, a piece of cloth awakened shortly beforehand but now
marooned at your feet, torn away from the long-distance hauler's
plush mascot cadaver, gummy from the air, snotty from the mist,
waved loose from the window of the driver's cab, intended for
you as its waving flashes in the rear-view mirror, now stuck in
place at this point in your life as currently extant, as it is here and
now before you, Doctor Webern, yes, that's right, perhaps at
pains—making a special effort, that is—to show that slip of paper,
the slip of paper from that distance, waving back toward you that
lightsnotted, illegible scrap, and then this wingbeat of a cloth
woven from a carrier pigeon, all fluttered out, plucked naked as
an absolutely final farewell flung at the feet of your pavement
figure, sadly stuck, lightquiversmiling, twitching its last in the
gridlocked emptiness of the cleared-out street, dejected and
bleak in the doorway of a dwellingvacated stairwellmounting
somber shadowing.

On looking out through a blind window as you surveyed everything around you during the final tour of inspection you con-
ducted through your vacated apartment in Vienna, already
rented again, yes, through that gray spot standing out from your
now former apartment, Doctor Webern, a spot breaking out from
the wall of your erstwhile building, additionally accessible from
that point on to your ensuing wallview-befogged scrutiny, Doctor
Webern, watching the moving van, though it's already out of
view, following with your eyes its journey as it goes gliding crosscountry and sliding Pragueward, riding then abiding stock still,
pulling up on one certain street, which, peculiarly enough, closely resembles your street in Vienna and, more surprisingly, your
building and its entryway there in Vienna, as does the transpar-

ently opened casement window opposite as well, the one you're looking out of, observing everything from there while it's all looking back in at you from the opened blind window (you're looking into your future apartment in Prague, Doctor Webern, oh yes, take a good look, a better look, a best look if you can, look windowwalledup, wallinward outward across country, look wallinward gapfree as made accessible to you, look inward enwindowed there, with your overexactness, Doctor Webern), then you might possibly, might just possibly see there—yes, there—you might possibly see yourself, hunkered down there at the blind window, looking out crosscountry from there and back to here at yourself, from there to here and back to Prague—it's as simple as that—oh yes, and then back from Prague to Vienna, hunkered down by the window, in turn then looking here and back from Vienna and outward to Prague and then back here one more time and—what? you don't want to hear about it in so much detail, you say?—why didn't you say so right away?—you'd rather have just gone on dreading it, you mean?—that's not what you want, though?—and that's why you're now looking away from the window there?—is that the reason why?!—perhaps because you would (as well you should, too) once again wave to yourself, all the way from out there, from Prague. Looking back in at yourself across country through the blind window there, looking back wallhunkered from there down into the street in front of the house in Prague (though perhaps you shouldn't, after all)—you composed nothing at all this past winter, and when you don't compose you don't exist—so wouldn't it be better, then, to compose at least something beforehand, here in Vienna, before you set off for Prague, so that in Prague you can really exist—but whether or no, Doctor Webern, don't you see your furniture being unloaded there, right now, the whole street here in Prague little by little growing jampacked with your furniture, blocking the view completely; don't you see that? Or maybe you'd rather say practically nothing—that's all right, too—since gradually each individual item is going through the front door, stairwellmounting, vanishing into your supposed future apartment, behind the blind window there in Prague, again opened casementwise inward, inthrust, its comprehensivenessblocking room concealment behind the tossed-out escape of your eye, secured in mortar twilight, widening out the spot—by smashing down plaster and rough-cast—in the limetrickling precipitation, to be anticipated sooner rather than later, and heavier rather than lighter, of a wallplaster streetdemolishing storm mortarlightningflashflaringly pounded loose from the memoryroofs of all these houses, looking enough alike to confuse them, and from the furylitter torrents of your layeredinstoriesunleashing stairwells, under the staircaserailing gradient of their rockslidescreespirals—so now off to the Franz Josef Station and into the post office, just before departing for Prague, to send a hasty telegram to Prague instructing the head of the moving company not to have your furniture removed from the van in Prague but to have everything, all of it, hauled back Viennawards instead without being unloaded —

when you yourself are finally in Prague, how smoothly it all went, Doctor Webern, and you finally meet once more with Herr Zemlinksy, who walks with you all through the city and shows you all the attractions, but then, unexpectedly and in person, you happen upon your furniture right out on the street, and it's laid out so as to block the way into and through the street, which is narrow—you watch the van driver first stuff into a pocket of his overalls a telegram he's only now received but already read and then make a very definite signal to one of the other movers, while you, on the other hand, are thanking Herr Zemlinsky for his exceptionally liberal offer, for the generous good will he is just in the process of manifesting to you—anything even remotely like it never ever having been bestowed on you in any such way from any quarter whatever, really and truly never—but what is it, Doctor Webern, the general music director is asking—you're at such a loss, yes you are, at a loss—but yet you find your way clear to mentioning the fears mounting inside you like the upthrust of a high mountain range, and you now explain your fear of once more not being able to compose anything this coming winter, of not being able to get to your composing here at all, Herr General Music Director, but when I don't compose I don't exist, please understand, Zemlinsky, that when I don't feel myself inside myself, neither as something working inside me nor as something new coming into being within me, when that last hope is only something stolen from a pawn shop instead of really belonging to me, when I can't even feel *that* inside me, Herr General Music Director, in the shape of my very last hope—and it's now died away again—then I don't exist, Herr General Music Director,

then there is no such person as me; after all, how do you feel
when you want to compose a piece but they don't let you, they
hold you back, how does that make you feel, Herr General Music
Director?
One hundred crowns, Zemlinsky replied; are one hundred
crowns too low a salary for you? That would really be a shame,
because I wasn't able to get any more out of them—not even for
you, Doctor Webern, was I able to get more; that amount is
keyed to the highest possible figure attainable on the salary scale,
which mandatorily applies to you as well as everyone else.
But when something isn't working inside me, you clearly explain
in reply, then I feel—both within myself and outside my own skin
as well—well-nigh incapable of taking up any work and therefore
in essence out of work. Do you undertand? Or not?
No, he says, not completely; Zemlinsky is now talking to you,
Herr Doctor, trying over and over to assure you of the absolutely
secure patronage his presence here puts him in a position to ex-
tend to you—but all this furniture here, he suddenly says, what's
it doing here, Doctor Webern, do you understand what is going
on with all these household goods and items of décor that look as
if they're going to furnish the whole street? Can you perhaps explain to whom such objects could possibly belong as were first
carried up—just to get the exercise—all the way to an apartment
on the top floor and then immediately carried back down, as
though a moving company would plan a self-contained furniture
moving event, not just to get the exercise but also to enhance the
professional competence of its newest employees by having the
furniture hauled up and then hauled right back down before you
even have a chance to pay the moving company—the men have
just now pulled up—for the trip here and before they can even
think of packing up everything again in preparation for moving it
all back? Don't you see those poor men there, Doctor Webern,
imagining that they're the victims of a mistake or of negligence
on the part of the boss? don't you see it that way? if you were to
ask me, the first thing I'd say is that we're watching unfold right
before our eyes yet one more of those cases—tragically growing
more and more frequent of late—in which confusion arising from
incredibly sloppy writing of an address leads to disastrous out-
comes. What do you think?

Why is he so worried about my furniture, you ask yourself, Doctor Webern; why is Zemlinsky bombarding me with questions
about the furniture? and you resolve—in accordance with your
belief that he's according your furniture excessive interest—to
give no answer, at least not yet, avoiding the issue by reverting to
the topic of his generosity and how nice it is of him and how sorry you are to have taken up so much of his time and effort re-
garding the business at hand, about which he has gone to so very
much trouble and for which you expressly want to thank him; a
hundred crowns, Herr General Music Director, a hundred
crowns, nowhere was I ever offered so much, which is too bad,
and my family really would be much better off here!
Ah yes, and how happy it makes him, the general music director
answers, to welcome with open arms your final, definite decision
to accept, Doctor Webern, dear friend, but unfortunately there
was just no getting more than a hundred crowns out of them; just
consider, though, the difference between this offer and all your
previous musical posts in other places, and just think, too, no
more crappy operettas like *Försterlieschen*, *Dollarprinzessin*,
Autoliebchen, and other such trash—no, now you can work on
Parsifal, for example, plus the hundred crowns, Doctor Webern!
Well of course it's *Parsifal* that especially tempts you at the moment, but you nevertheless reply to Zemlinksy only by expressing
your hope that he won't think too very ill of you, while reacting
sadly out of a belief that you may have behaved badly toward him
by making him trudge all through the streets of Prague with you
for hours, which ended up in a happenstantial trudge to this very
spot, Herr Zemlinsky, and so you say (and this is verbatim): But
if something doesn't come out of me soon, then it's possible that
nothing more will ever come out, and I'm afraid of that, Herr
General Music Director; please understand, Zemlinsky, if nothing more ever comes out of me, then presumably I'm no longer
even here, Zemlinsky, but gone, vanished right down through the
sidewalk, this minute, faded away to nothing, probably not even
standing here even now, as I speak; tell me, Herr General Music
Director, am I still standing here or not? please tell me, or rather
no, don't say anything, but reach out instead; yes, please reach
out to me so you can reach an understanding about how much of
me is still here (which I bet is nothing); yes, please reach out,

take hold, reach out to me and grab hold, please, Herr General
Music Director, so that you can feel how much of me is still here!
And Zemlinsky does in fact reach out to you, Doctor Webern,
stretches out his arm to you, Doctor Webern—finally—and so
you're thinking: he's reaching out to me and not pointing to the
furniture, and: yes, you're taking hold at last, you say, and so
you'll soon discover for yourself that there's practically nothing
of me here; oh yes, I've probably disappeared altogether, I'm not
here at all any more; before you instead, Herr General Music Director, is the outline of the shadow my former figure used to cast,
you'll see soon enough!
And while he is in fact reaching over to you or out to you, something happens to you, Doctor Webern, something enduring, if also shrouded, shrouding you somehow in any case, as you're saying please take hold and he at that very moment is indeed reaching over to you there, or seems to be reaching out to you, yes,
more or less reaching for your hand with his, Doctor Webern,
something comes over you, off to the side and beneath your skin,
albeit through and through, a slight bodydissipatingshiverbrief
stumble or flutter off to the side such that you in any event back
away from his hand—still in process of reaching out to yours—
back down, back off, back up, or is it more along the lines of a
stumble, for just a quick second, tripping over the uneven stones
patterned on the sidewalk, that makes you back away from him,
slipping and sliding a bit, back away, skitter, slither past the Herr
General Music Director reaching his hand out to take hold of
you, though instead of grasping you, of getting a grasp on you, he
actually reaches out to the air next to you, misses you, so don't
you see, Herr General Music Director, there's nothing left of me,
I'm not even here, so now do you finally understand?!
There's nothing more about me to grasp or hold, all drained off,
so take a look down below, down below street level—yes indeed!—under the pavement is where you'll most likely find me!
So you'll have to tear up the sidewalk, right on this very spot!
And oh how heavily the paving stones press down on my chest,
pushing me down, down, away from the sphere of earth, and
then farther down yet, into the planet, getting me out of the way,
that's right, and I can slowly feel myself draining away once and
for all from this point in my life! So go ahead and remove the top
layer of the street, Herr General Music Director; go on and start

lifting away the paving stones! You'll find me right underneath
this spot, yes you will; if you will right now discreetly grope
around under the surface, you'll be able to feel me there, that is if
I haven't yet once and for all oozed away, down, down, down—
that's the reason, or that's one of the reasons why I can't stay
here, why I can't come to Prague in the first place, that is, can't
come to work with you in Prague, Herr General Music Director,
because I'm not even here—and in order to be able to stay here,
I'd first, you see, have to clamber back up from down there, back
up from the center of the earth to this pavement sidewalk in Prague on which you're standing. Don't you see me, Herr General
Music Director, digging my way back up through the surface of
the pavement, see how grueling that is for me, just like a gigantic
mole, don't you think, and how I've now burrowed my way back
up, Herr General Music Director, and am just now standing before you again, ready for grasping, somehow unfathomably
emerged from fathoms deep, as you well know, suddenly quite
visible to you again, or am I wrong? Wait, I just have to shake the
dust off, best to just knock the dirt off my coat, knock it to the
ground, you see, but this earthly dirt can't be shaken off entirely,
and the lining here is all sticky with clay in some places, but nonetheless here I am standing on the surface once again, never
mind that I'm a little woozy around the edges just now, or maybe
I should say noticeably blurry, but beyond all doubt just as noticeably there for the seizing hold of, as you can fathom, good
friend Zemlinsky; I'm graspable again, practically equipped with
handles, and I'm ready to be seized hold of at any time and above
all to be grasped, to be gripped at once, oh yes indeed!! just look
at me now, quite graspably graspable from close up once more—
or no?—all you have to do is reach out finally and take hold, dear
Herr von Zemlinksy, so please take a good grip at last, before it
will yet once again have grown too late!
So why doesn't he grab hold, you ask yourself, Doctor Webern,
and you're quite right, because the question arises yet once again
as to why he is yet once again seizing on the wrong direction as
he points, inasmuch as the motion of his hand movement has
turned away from you, unfortunately, moving the opposite way,
in fact, in the direction of all that furniture standing out on the
street in Prague, blocking the way for anyone wanting to enter
the building, all congested around the entrance; instead of reach-

ing out to you, Zemlinsky again grasps hold of air, so naturally he
misses you and points to your furniture—Doctor Webern, he
says, look at the furniture there, all this furniture has just now
arrived, hasn't it, just a short while ago, as they say, very recently, but instead of being unloaded and moved entranceinward
stairwellupward, it has now quite unexpectedly turned back in
crabwise motion, reciprocally escaped, oh yes, houseoutward
fallbackwithdrawpushback pushed back out with pushiness,
pushing along pushily, and how, doorbackpush pushed back,
backedoutwise back out on the street, backshoved, moved back—
clearly loaded back, however that may be, even though the moving van has just now arrived, Doctor Webern, all that stuff only
now arrived, unloaded just now, wasn't it, all those goods and
chattel vanished into the house and now again through the front
door and onto the street, now so abruptly excrementated house-
outwards—well how else to say it, Doctor Webern, would you by
chance understand any better way?!—but tell me, please, who
does all this furniture belong to? Are you of the belief that anyone else in the building, in which it is yet hoped you will be residing for quite some time to come, has at his or her disposal this
kind of live furniture, as it were, autonomous of motion and
practically self-transporting? What? Did you say you? To you? I
certainly wouldn't have expected that would be your answer, and
I altogether fail to understand why your furniture is leaving you
all alone here in Prague, hardly having arrived than it is again
without you, Doctor Webern, your very own furniture making
off, abandoning your future lodgings with a hop, skip, and a
jump, off all those pieces go without you, Doctor Webern, taking
care of themselves all on their merry own and very own, shipping
themselves off and away from here, getting out of Prague at once,
Doctor Webern, but why do they so dislike Prague, of all places,
that's inexplicable, Doctor Webern, or do you know of any cause
for such discontent; well maybe it's owing to an altogether extraordinary condition of going against nature, since we all know
Prague to be one of those cities that's home to any and every kind
of prop or frame awakened to life and famed in myth and legend,
starting with scarecrows and other objects cavorting around on
their own, such as beanpoles that have run away from their gar-
dens, all the way to the metalgratingpoultry wreneagled fogbird-
brained plumeplummeted barbedwirefeathered rustwinged skit-

terers from the scrap iron foundry—and so on and so on, Doctor
Webern; so why? and I'm asking you to just say right out with
ruthless honesty, please, if you know more about these things
than I do.
It's because I can't come to Prague, Herr General Music Director,
and in order for me to say all that to you, however quickly, but at
least in person, is why I earlier undertook to travel here to Prague, in order to tell you all this in person, to tell you—but only after all my furniture had been taken out of my apartment in Vienna and transported here to Prague, only right after which there
came to me the saving thought of not being able to come to Prague at all, whereupon I immediately went to the Franz Josef Station to catch the train to Prague, to come and see you, so that I
could explain it all to you in person, after I had previously (so as
not to have to even look at my furniture in Prague), even before
the train departed, sent off a telegram here, to my future address,
directing that my furniture should not so much as be unloaded
upon its arrival here but was to be shipped back to Vienna in a
twinkling, hoping thereby not to have to set eyes on any of that
junk any more, all of which, as far as I'm concerned, should have
vanished back to Vienna even before my arrival here in Prague,
so that I would be spared having to be confronted in person with
any of that junk; but talk about premature hope while on my way
to Prague, or on my way to anywhere, for that matter, because
now that I'm here, it seems to me, strangely enough, that I haven't really arrived, not really, but that I'm somehow still traveling, even now as I speak, sitting square in the middle of my train
compartment, the coach perhaps uncoupled and stuck somewhere, strayed onto a side track nearby and I possibly stuck
headlong on the section between Vienna and Prague, all in order
to say to you first and foremost, Herr General Music Director—
that I can't come to you in Prague, that I can't stay here, and all
of that is what I've been hoping to try to explain to you in person,
you see.
So then the General Music Director asks you some questions—
where you intend to go from here if you're not going to stay
here—not remaining will make you remaindered, after all—so
where exactly it is you're thinking of going from here is what he
wants to know, Doctor Webern, and also what other questions he
should be asking you now; the answer you give him, however, is

that you have no idea what to tell him, neither about yourself—about your own person, that is—or about how to proceed next; so this is exactly what you say: I must go to that place to which I felt drawn by coming here; and you make further mention of that newly invented time realm in some setting not yet precisely ascertainable, having become audible to you only a short time ago, situated somewhat farther aloft, some place up above where a few passably comfortable rooms would be offered to your compositions, and my saying that gives you reason enough to see why I can't stay here in Prague, Herr Zemlinsky, although right now there's nothing I'd rather be able to do than to work here with you; after all, that's something I've always dreamed about, at least since we came to know each other personally; and then you go on to explain: But if I were actually to stay here with you in Prague, then I would in a twinkling once more have oozed away at this same spot, down past the surface layer of the sidewalk, just as before, and would become backundercellardepaved, earthinward far far away, deepdownwardasphalted, and so, as far as it affects you, my remaining here—and this is exactly what I've been wanting to say the whole time: I would be of no use to you whatever in case I were to stay but would nonetheless have oozed away down deep, as if through a drainpipe planetmidpointgutterlengthed—would thus make it only *seem* as if you had me on hand, transparent, just as before, standing straight in front of you, but yet not really, so that it would not be possible even to grasp hold of what looks like my body with your hands (can you grasp it?), I in fact having grown only all the more unreachable if I were to remain here, and so all that would remain of me would be a kind of hollow silhouetteskinned puppet from a shadow play, right through which it is entirely possible you could reach, just as before, reaching through and past me into thin air and not able to take me in hand at all—in short, it's altogether probable that I'm not even here, dear Herr General Music Director.

But look here, Doctor Webern, the General Music Director answers, your furniture's now been loaded back onto the truck—that certainly went fast—and is ready to be driven off, and—at least I think so—the van driver is smiling, because he has just now realized that the furniture itself is the contracting party, and he is coming over to us in reference to his need to request more

exact information of you on behalf of your furniture, which re-
quires additional details—
Excuse me, Doctor Webern, you hear the driver say, excuse me,
Doctor Webern: he now recognizes you and is walking up to you,
and you hear him asking where in Vienna the furniture . . . that is
back to Vienna, of course that much is clear, but then where to in
Vienna, Doctor Webern, exactly where, probably back to the old
address—
No, you reply, that wouldn't work, it's impossible, in fact, because the apartment in Vienna was rented back out long ago and
so isn't available any more—
Well then exactly where in Vienna, where should I take the con-
tents, and it really is a valid question, to which you, Doctor Webern, give the driver a very simple and very proper answer: anywhere you want, just drive away with all this junk here, just plain
drive off, take all this stuff home with you, yes, that's it, and by
the time I'm back in Vienna I'll have come up with some suitable
address, but no, that won't do after all; I apologize, how could I
ask such a thing of you, so what you could do is take all the furniture to some temporary furniture waiting room in Vienna; after
all, something like that has to exist somewhere in Vienna, a place
just standing by somewhere and waiting for such lost objects,
items, and articles for furnishing, outfitting, and equipping dwelling places to be granted their temporary residency permits; well,
one way or another, please just simply take all this stuff to the
baggage claim department at the South Station or to the West
Station, or simply to somewhere or another, because basically I
just flat out do not want to see any of this junk any more or be in
any way forced to come across any of it anywhere—
finally the truck drives away, and Zemlinsky asks, well where do
you want to live here in Prague, Doctor Webern, because you'll
surely be staying for a few days anyway, and in fact I'm specifically requesting that you stay for at least a few days, if not longer;
you could spend those few days upstairs, in your new apartment,
yes, the very one you no longer intend to settle into but on which
the rent has been paid for a few months in advance, so wouldn't
those rooms upstairs be at your disposal for a few days, at least?
No, you reply to the General Music Director, no, there's no
chance whatever of my even crossing the threshold of, let alone
occupying, some hypothetical apartment subsisting only in the

subjunctive; it would be too risky to dwell for even a brief time up there on the top floor, under the roof, no, that just would not do at all, not even if I were selfsubjunctively to confine myself to two hypothesisrooms; it would be even more impossible, even more entirely out of the question, because it would thereupon be entirely possible to get somehow stuck up there or to be unreachably, inaccessibly trapped by the spatial caverns of an uninhabitable roomhypothesis of the hypothetical rooms of all the spatial coverings trapped undwellably up there within their walls—roomlost waylost, despaced, locked in, sealed amidst invisible rooms between rooms, locked in and locked out, then roomejected locked out, timelessnessed, from said point on each and every bit of whatever remnants of rooms have been able to remain for you turned out, outroomed, and so you might be thankful for the very final broomroomencounter amidst an uninhabitably liveddead patch of air in the burned-out sky: but the way you really answer the General Music Director's question (where to now?) is much easier than before: I don't know, Herr General Music Director, but there is one thing I know for sure, which is that we can't keep standing at this spot even a single second longer without our immediately, I mean in a twinkling, becoming rooted to the spot, even now more and more impenetrable, soon past the point of no return, tougher and tougher in the thickening air, without our ever being able to get away from here again; come, Zemlinksy, let's finally move on, at least a short ways away from here, though there's nothing like getting away altogether, so I'd like to ask you simply to come to the station with me and to wait until the train that's to take me back to Vienna actually departs, so that when I've arrived back in Vienna but am not sure that I really have arrived in Vienna and really and truly am in Vienna, I can call you from there to ask you if I really did depart from Prague and if you should happen to be in a position to bear witness that I really did depart from Prague for Vienna, and that much at least will be certain, if nothing else is.

Thank God there's a war coming, Doctor Webern, the First World War, an operetta war, and you enlist for it voluntarily, because people have confused the whole world for an operetta, for which reason it's altogether mandatory that this war will have to begin by destroying operetta—

You may be in the last contingent of those liable for military service, Doctor Webern, but that puts you in a category grandly
called *Landsturmpflichtige*—those obligated to storm the land,
that is—and in that capacity you are charged with showing every
gust of wind its way through the land, with observing every storm
down to the most exact detail, and with gathering into bundles
and directing toward their respective targets, with the artillery-
level precison of typhoons' eyes calculated in advance, every
glance from any and all assembled hurricanes—so yes indeed,
Doctor Webern, as you notice, theater and military operations
exhibit great similarity, and these experiences will stand you in
very good stead, especially during chorus rehearsals; the only
important point is that everyone take it all as seriously as possible and that you yourself be prepared to explain everything in the
most businesslike manner, every apparent drill, because after all
the whole thing makes eminently good sense, doesn't it?—
You've got to see to it that the world of operetta, which if un-
checked will turn the entire population of the globe into mindless
zombies, comes crashing down from its grimy perch above the
stage, up in the fly gallery, and make it an explosion of grime if
you have to, Doctor Webern, an explosion throughout the whole
world, even if all the roseate heavens filled with a thousand violins have to catch on fire and the flaming fiddles fall on everybody's head and all the blazing operetta angels with their fake
flame costumes go plummeting into the sea, Doctor Webern, for
all of that would count as part of the *Kulturkampf*, a classic clash
of cultures, wouldn't it?—
Debussy going after the imitators of Wagner with a knife —
an enraged Maurice Ravel driving a truck loaded with explosives
into the *Hofburg*, the Imperial Palace in Vienna —
and Hofmannsthal opening fire on Maeterlinck —
not only do our soil and our homeland have to be defended, but
also the culture and art of the West, now under challenge from
every side, so that wherever you look the intellectual and spiritual heroes of the nations, such as Richard Strauss and Hans
Pfitzner (goes without saying), are being excused from military
service, though Schönberg was called up for the army soon
enough, whereas the worst operetta parasites, take Lehár for example, are exempted, Doctor Webern—do you hear me, Lehár,
that bastard—and have you forgotten that every real war starts

with hastily hatched henhouse haranguings, chicken-coop con-
trivings and connivings leading to cockfights that never stay on
the level of popular entertainment, however, because the fire in
the operetta sky has set the real sky on fire, too, whereupon it
burns up and comes toppling down, sinking into the sea; finally
you've had a bit of success, your Opus 1 has at last been performed to good effect in several European cities, but how long
ago that Opus 1 is and how far past it you are now; even so, the
composers in Europe all make up and come to Vienna to visit the
Verein für Musikalische Privataufführungen, the Society for
Private Musical Perfomances, which you founded, and in the Socialist Art Center you achieved the singular success, after found-
ing the Workers' Symphony Concerts, of performing Gustav
Mahler's "Symphony of a Thousand," with a chorus of working-
class singers, with greater magnificence than had ever been
heard up to then, but only after you had undertaken the obligation of teaching every individual chorus member every single
note by whistling and singing it to them, because these singers
from the working class, musical illiterates all, were in no position
to learn how to read music—yet and still, the very best that came
out of the First World War is *Wozzeck*, that opera by your best
friend Alban Berg—

you hear that, Raymond, where are you, don't hide, one of Doctor
Webern's friends is writing a whole opera about you, *Wozzeck*,
but you're one better, because you don't have to stab your wife,
as in the opera; you finally got rid of her a while ago so you could
drink in peace, drink your way into the drink or let the Atlantic
drink you, simply waiting for the surging billows to engulf you;
virtue, says Wozzeck, is something for upper-crust people, edu-
cated people, you hear that, Raymond, it must be a beautiful
thing, this virtue, but you're just a poor devil, so don't hide,
you're lying in wait for yourself everywhere anyway before you
get to some other place, before you get wise to your own self,
catch yourself completely by surprise and then quickly take to
your heels, off to the next place, from which you then have to
move on to yet the next point of your gradual demise, taking with
a gulp between two gulps of air a few gulps from a bottle through
whose drunken swill you trudge and stagger in hopes of reaching
a place from which there's no more going away—

it might have been something like this: you open the door, which breaks loose and almost flutters away in the burning autumn wind of evening, by which you're blinded, you can't see anything but this muzzle flash right opposite you, then you hear a shot or an explosion from over that way, so you ask yourself who could be shooting at you, and of course you shoot back—
but then where did those bullet holes in the house wall come from, and how could you shoot a house in the wall, since you, stepping out the main door of that house as you left it, are supposed to have fired in the opposite direction from the house, whereas you left open the front door, hysterically nagging and shouting, because it came upfastened from its hinges and fled from its frame, smashed all to pieces after it soared aloft and away far above you, flying over the countryside in the horizon-beach of the commencing night —
do you see the trees, how they thrust upward arrowlike out of the ground, shoot up into the air and arrow a path skyward, furiously taking precise aim with the points of their crowns, and stick smack in the middle of some point in the air above you, suddenly stopping but yet continuing to quiver to a standstill in a great rage, because they would much have preferred to keep on hurtling further, out into outer space? But there's always something, if not one thing then another, trying to hold them down, even below earth's surface, like an arrow that stays stuck in the bow when it's fired, and then there's another one, and it even starts to come apart somehow, barksplintered, woodrottensaw-dustpowdercrumbled, falling earthward from the sky, drawn back down and buried anew; you watch out that you're not standing someplace where somebody shoots you upward arrow-like, right under your soles, along with himself, and nails you high above to the sky; you'd like that, though, wouldn't you?—

but over there in Europe, Raymond, bad times will soon be coming back, Mussolini's already at it, in Germany Hitler's coming, and in Vienna the elegant Dollfuss sashays into Parliament and dissolves it: you really could pay a visit to Alban Berg and before he dies—which will be quite soon now—thank him for his opera about you, about a man like you . . . "an insect," he tells the doctor, do you hear that, he never even saw it happen, hardly even felt the sting, feels as if he's been skewered by an insect, and

money's grown very tight, "I'm probably going to have to sell the house in the woods pretty soon," he tells the doctor, and the car, too, unfortunately; there aren't any more royalties coming in from Germany since my works were banned, Alban goes on to say, swept aside, we're being swept aside, Anton; I'm not doing well, you'll conduct the premiere of the violin concerto in Barcelona, Krasner will play it—he commissioned it—I'm suffering from a long drawn-out case of blood poisoning, transfiguration in death treated in the violin concerto, it's a requiem, but not for me, Anton, it's for Manon Gropius, not for me, no, you can't really mean that either, she never even quite made it to twenty —
Schönberg's going to America for good—he's not of Germanic extraction, they've kicked him out of every place they could—but Doctor Webern absolutely must prevent that, what's he supposed to do without his great master and teacher, some kind of leftover all alone over there at that, Raymond, do you hear, the acoustical world champion from Austria is coming to you in America, perhaps even straight to you, to this provincial spot, meantime turned so desolate and bleak, in that New World of yours! So why don't you come along too, Doctor Webern? It would be better for you: Doctor Webern's great role model Gustav Mahler set a precedent, he went there a long time ago, after they hounded him out of Vienna, snapping at his heels, chasing him and shooing him across the Atlantic, but then he left again quite soon, didn't he, traveling back to himself so he could die in his Old World —
things are going downhill, Mussolini is at it, Hitler's coming, and at home our own elegant Dollfuss sashays into Parliament and dissolves it—Raymond, come on and sing a song like one of Wozzeck's or like the one Marie, whom he stabbed, sings to the little boy, come on, sing, Raymond, sing:
steering the sailboat
sample drinks already finished
highseaworthy light little boat
rainbowcolored highaltitude railroad
two more drinks yet:
a cup of frozen grog
and a glass of boiling ice water —
Who is flinging these words, these gestures in air, these twisted sunbeamgrimaces, this whispered chatter of microscopically re-

duced sheetlightning signalflashes at the heads of you and Doctor Webern?—surely you must sometimes want to know that.

Who is sowing such symbols, twice twining, such calling, two timelessed fields of vision twinned in time to be untwisted?

A shake of the head, even about light at a loss, can offer you—though rarely—an answer only hinted at.

And it comes perhaps in syllables at best, scraps of syllables of the kind that coaxes out of the forgotten blinding of a shattered typhoon's eye an unknown shadowbreath, secret blacklightheart of all those nights that are prevented by it from occurring: coaxes and blows through forests and over villages, cities, all scattered through rooms, and the very sounds of which compose themselves into such words, sentences, and stories, into such rumors as no one can ever know anything of, certainly, but with which everyone nevertheless purports at times to have been familiar all along and claims to be precisely verifiable.

But from whom should such sounds—buzzing, humming, ringing—originate and inward into whose heads be steered, in the cavities of whose hearing (yours, for instance) should they adhere to the eardrums and then fall asleep, so as to wait from then on—cocooned forever, as petrified, dreamdissolved nests in the chambers of memory—for the end of all thinking, so as then and only then to escape, to vanish again by slipping away, with whatever thoughts might be remaining, to somewhere, anywhere, like invisibly transparent clouds of insects?—All you have to do is ask the words themselves. But even in case many of the words heard your question and understood it and found themselves thereupon in a position to give you some kind of an answer in some kind of way—maybe mealymouthed—were to discover themselves disposed to mutter something unintelligible as if to themselves but really to you, as though you were worthy to be told secrets: even in that case what you need to know is that words themselves would often rather fall back on lying, as they so notoriously understand how to do; but most of the time these words have no mouth, and they don't care to inform you whose mouth is supposed to have uttered them at one time; nor, once they have been spoken, from whose lips, as from a diving board, you have been flung down to the deep, if not the depths, flung off your base, debased; nor do words want to know what they mean to anyone or what kind of memoryforwardcrushing blindness

they may mashmeaningly draw behind them from whatever eye
may glimpse them; nor is there one single word that knows anything whatever about its meaning or any such thing as a meaning
at all, for that matter; nor does it want to hear anything about
that thing called memory, from which it allegedly escapes and
gets chased off, only to then, over and over, spend the winter
temporarily, as a fugitive, in the heads of strangers, from whom
the best that can be hoped for, however, is that some of the ear-
splitting sounds, as in a fierce draft or a crackling noise in the
head, would grow more or less audible and understandable (such
as when the doctor cleans out your ears)—oh yes, then you would
know quite a bit more than you do now, wouldn't you?! —

and you, Doctor Webern, are trying for the last time to keep
Schönberg from going to America; he just asked you to call him
by first name and by the friendly, intimate *"Du"* instead of the
formal *"Sie,"* which had been your unvarying form of address up
to now, and his asking you that is one of the greatest moments of
your life—"what's truly German," you explain to him, "has always
been better understood by Jews than by Germans themselves:
the primacy of German music, Arnold, the primacy of Western
culture, Arnold—to whom do we owe that if not to you; somebody's got to persuade Hitler how right and logical the twelve-
tone system is, Arnold, and why shouldn't it be you; who else, after all, and then everything will be all right again—imagine not
being able to recognize the unmistakable Germanness of your
music, of our music; nobody can remain that deaf, dumb, and
blind for very long: *"Entartet"?* "Degenerate"? You, Arnold? Me?
It's a misunderstanding, an untenable one, because isn't this system, Arnold, once it gains a foothold here in Austria, going to
lead to the triumph of the cultural aims for which we've been
fighting so long? Mahler, Arnold—just think—Mahler will finally
be understood!"—Oh yes, Doctor Webern, every letter carrier will
soon be whistling your scores, Doctor Webern, and out of the
deepest hole a cold wind will soon come whistling as well, so
watch out that you don't catch an awful cold, or do I mean a ca-
tarrh?—because what you have in mind is a catharsis, Doctor
Webern, an inner purification, that is, not one proceeding on the
outside only, and with giant steps to this point, continuing on
your way in twelve-league boots; you have in mind simply to an-

chor the rules of twelve-tone music by passing legislation making them compulsory, printing them as a preface to the Code of Civil Law throughout the whole world; so what you have in mind is simply that it would make for a new start—oh you mean a new *state*, one in which your scores would be whistled by even the simple man, one who doesn't command even the most primitive laws of grammar, never mind that the future of the world could depend on a comma correctly or incorrectly placed—to dig deep into the soil is what you have in mind, to turn the whole earth over with a plow—yes, all the way down to the ground water, which will then flood upward and overflow every land, changing them all into swamps where today every little pond and puddle cleans itself—that's it, isn't it?—and how wonderfully the swamps all glow at night, Doctor Webern, glowworms, phosphorescent wood, Doctor Webern, and all that without using even a single kilowatt of electrical current—thus the new mounts upward from undamaged primeval soil and transforms our planet into nothing but swampland, Doctor Webern, ours and all the other ones as well, however distant, and you can feel the air from them ever more clearly, Doctor Webern, oh yes, you can breathe again, can't you, you can very clearly feel *"Luft von anderen Planeten,"* as in that poem from Schönberg's string quartet, "air from other planets," that's what you can say to Schönberg as your conclusion, and you know, Arnold, when every letter carrier is whistling our scores, then we too will be able to be happy—but you'd better take another look around, Doctor Webern: Arnold isn't listening any more; he's gone all of a sudden.

And now the only thing left to do is visit Alban one last time in the hospital; he's afraid all he'll be able to write in the future are operettas, because the last transfusion they gave him contained only blood donated by a clothes-horse tenor from Sankt Pölten — and fear is all that remains to him now, stuck fast as it is among a group of moments lost and gone astray, fallen as if among notes, notes by you, Doctor Webern, ones he loved so much all throughout his life; Alban is talking about how sharp-pointed needle tones are sticking in him, to be borne off by needletone- points sticking in the stillness, Doctor Webern, no, not Alban, he can't be a mosquito jabbing into a silence, stuck fast in the un- ending stillness of transparent fly paper there in the middle of the sky and leaving behind for you only the violin concerto, of

which you're to give the premiere in Barcelona, and with an orchestra that's really quite good but assuredly not good enough for that piece, in spite of Pablo Casals, and, if in doubt, you'll have to interrupt the rehearsals to keep Alban's violin concerto from any chance of coming to grief, right at its first performance, through any fault of your own, because this much is certain, and it's something you learn from your very first look at the score: this violin concerto contains, probably at the end, a very decisive note, which, upon being played for the first time, will never come to a stop, and if the first performance, under your supervision, after all, should have to bear the responsibility, through your fault, for the coming to grief of this decisive note—one conceived by Alban—the very first time it sounds—no, that just must not and shall not happen, Doctor —
standing now before the orchestra, Doctor Webern, yes, you, and you have taken the resolve—here in Barcelona, and have accordingly requested the assistance of an interpreter, if need be—of working through Alban's violin concerto, if need be, right here and now, with every one of the musicians individually, note for note, each one in person, if need be:

Good morning, gentlemen, or should I say my sincere condolences, but for whom? of course for our deceased colleague Alban Berg, in whose memory we are now setting out to rehearse his last work, his violin concerto, it being in its turn a work he dedicated to the memory of an angel and called a requiem, circumstance having unfortunately compelled him to compose it as his own requiem, even if against his will—well, then, gentlemen, to the memory of an angel—andante—soft, very soft—piano—a soaring aloft—flight soaring aloft to a soaring in flight—once more from the beginning, please!
(What's being sounded in those first rising fifths, Doctor Webern, has to be broken off with no comment; I'm sure you feel the same)
No, gentlemen, not like that, please; as you perhaps know, it stands, proportionally speaking, in direct and indirect connection and misconnection, at one and the same time, as it were, to the treatment of an instrument, as it were, that is to what extent its mechanical sound can or cannot be kept at low volume—normal now, but sharp and clean, please!

(That's not much better, Doctor Webern; just put a stop to this
trash immediately)
How can I make myself best understood to you?
My best attempt to get at what I mean would sound something
like this, gentlemen: Not in this work only, the violin concerto by
Alban Berg, but here especially—though it pertains to all the rest
as well—we shouldn't even have to play the piece; the sound
must by all means be present before you even play it! You
mustn't even think of playing it before you hear it clearly, in your
own head, I mean, of course, and so I'm asking you not to let
your bodies and your whole physical being stand in the way of
the music, so to speak, while you're attempting to play it— now
once more, please!
(It doesn't sound, Doctor Webern, as if things were getting any
better; perhaps it would help if you called back to the musicians'
minds the dedication of the concerto—angel, Doctor Webern,
and other bird people; these Spaniards are Catholics through and
through, after all, so maybe it would help, and also if you were to
say the word in Spanish)
No, no, gentlemen; stop, it just won't do like this, I'm sorry to
say; let me ask you, the interpreter, if there isn't an equivalent in
Spanish for the word "angel"—what did you say?—how do you
say it?—how exactly?—"angel," you said, which is all well and
good, though you don't need to be saying it to me, but rather to
the people there—so, gentlemen, it isn't here, in the midst of our
surroundings, that we should be searching, but somewhere beyond, but as long as we're not in a state of grace, we'll more than
likely continue to search in vain; now bearing that in mind, start
over!
(These people just want to pick you up and carry you away now;
listen—they're going through the motions of playing, what they'd
like to demonstrate to you is that they are able to produce silence, so you need to go along with it and not feel in the least as if
you were being picked up and carried away)
Yes, gentlemen, that's very good! A flawless acoustic; do you hear
it?—may this total silence resound in all of us; and now do you
understand what I mean? No? Well, the way Schönberg puts it is
that at certain very definite times music can also be an exercise
for the deaf, meaning that no one among us needs to prove by
playing music that it exists; music doesn't need that; what a mis-

take, though; I just don't know, gentlemen, haven't we been
working well together this whole time, right from the beginning?—so my hope now is that we can all bend over the score together and let the first measures resound in our heads and then
from out of our heads, note for note; very intensive, and then we
would through sheer concentration on our part be in a position
to hear Alban's first few measures sounding from out of our
heads without ever touching a single instrument; or at least to
produce a silence which will prepare Alban's first tones in such a
way that we are in a position to play them for the first time, as
they emerge from that silence, on and with our instruments—so
now note by note, but if at all possible without sliding your
chairs!
(If they don't hear anything by now, Doctor Webern, then they're
truly musicians struck stone-deaf, at least in a figurative sense;
but you are probably hearing only this frozen silence)
Do you hear the silence, gentlemen—do you? But right away
you're damaging it again for me; you probably don't *want* to understand me correctly. This morning on your way to rehearsal
you all surely must have seen those red and black flags hanging
all over the city. If we keep going this way, we'll have to hold the
rest of our rehearsals in jail, if we're not all shot, that is—now
once more from the beginning, please —
(No, Doctor Webern, there's nothing that can be done, just put a
stop to it at once)
Oh well, gentlemen, perhaps that's it—we never see anything
through to a complete finish, so let's try just one more time: not
the finishing touches, we'll settle for the not-quite-finished
touches—or on second thought no, not on my watch, no, this way
just won't do!

Better, Doctor Webern, to stay in your room but still keep secret
hold of the chief supervisory capacity for the performance of Alban's concerto, which you've turned over to Hermann Scherchen;
up to now everything's been going outstandingly, if not always
exactly the way it should, Alban's sounds an echo from the shadow of a silence, an echo from a rock face, a sound there for the
hearing before a single note is ever shouted at the rock face on
the mountain heights, a sound given off by the echoing rock face
itself without its ever having to be disturbed; and now the last

note, the one that will never stop, the one with which Alban
composed in advance the echo, sounded in advance, of that insect that got him later; now that note is sounding, yes, for the
first time, and it really and truly doesn't come to a stop, not ever;
so everything once again did go well at the last minute, a minute
in which it's clear to you, Doctor Webern, that many will have
cause to be thankful to Alban for this violin concerto, many who,
without the music played this way after everything had once
more come to grief, didn't make do as easily as they would have
with Alban's help; for that matter, he's helping you as well, now
that everything has come to grief again for you, helping you to go
on, which you do by simply continuing, first and foremost, and at
all times, to listen to that last note of Alban's, which continues to
sound and which will always be with you —

And you, Raymond—you're paralyzed by those final, buzzing
notes of the concerto, which, as they go flying away from the violin, will never come to a stop and will swoop down on you from
the sky, transformed into invisible insects, singing while stinging
and making your blood curdle—
a notable success, Doctor Webern, but don't you realize even a
little that you almost prevented the whole thing from happening?—What's that you're saying? You think you didn't prevent
anything; instead, it was you who saved the performance? Really? So what you're saying is that because you didn't walk out
right after the first rehearsal you saved the premiere?!—The sea
is listening to you, Doctor Webern, do you hear, when Alban's
widow was pleading with you through the locked door of your
hotel room to hand over the score so that the orchestra could finally rehearse it with Hermann Scherchen, and didn't you at first
want to save Alban's concerto altogether from such musicians as
those, preferring to let it remain unplayed? Excuse me? You
saved Alban's concerto nonetheless, you say? But weren't you
afraid at first that an actual performance would be the death of
Alban's concerto? Tell me, Doctor Webern, aren't you sometimes
afraid of muscial notes?!—Of wrong notes, of course, you say;
very well, then; the next notes, the correct ones, that will become
audible to you, though that won't be for ten years yet, are waiting
for you at the entrance to a dark corridor in Mittersill; in ten
years, Doctor Webern, and loneliness until then, Doctor Webern,

privations and sacrifices, humiliations and mortifications—ten
years, ten minutes, ten seconds —

Don't you ever ask yourself, Raymond, why you'll never quite
manage to effect a full exchange with Doctor Webern? Don't you
think he might well refuse to take your place? To stand in for
you? Don't fool yourself, we could be talking about an insinua-
tion here—look, over on the other side of the street, he's standing
right there, oh yes, hasn't Doctor Webern brought the cello for
you?—and vanishing into the huge building, by the back entrance, yes, oh how lucky that you have your new job and understood how to place yourself directly across from this huge hotel,
where they almost crowned you as general music director of the
kitchen before the war, before your call-up for military service
took you away and shipped you out to Europe—what business
does Doctor Webern have in there?—You have to find him, you
need a good friend, you need him urgently, a partner to explain
everything to you, to do everything with you; how would it be if it
were Doctor Webern? Go inside, follow him, and if it should turn
out that he's your adversary, then you have to kick him out at
once! —
Yet higher up, up into the mountain heights, Doctor Webern, up
into the attic of the atmosphere, Doctor Webern, do you hear this
burning fire of sound everywhere throughout this whole area
around the *Großvenediger* and the other high mountains?
That's living music, those are microscopic sound beings, living
things made of musical tones inhabiting the whole atmosphere,
where you, too, Doctor Webern, have a room high up in the rarified air, where you get through the winter, the lonely privations
of your most recent years, together with the sound beings you
conceived; Alban's concerto is there as well, over there, that
huge, invisible, transparent sound bird slowly soaring past up
above, wandering, orbiting the atmosphere day and night like an
invisible constellation—
Listen, Raymond, it might have been something like this: you
open the door quite speedily, even though there's a whole decade
placed at your disposal for setting your hand to the door: there
he is, standing outside, in front of the house, and he seems to
want to go in, and so you've opened the door for him in a friendly
way for him to step inside, good evening, and you want to reach

out to shake hands with him, or he with you, but just as you go to place your fingers into his hand, or—the other way around—he his into yours, you've suddenly burned your fingers on the glowing match he's putting up to his mouth to set alight his cigar; well, that's taking things too far, so all that's left is fire! And fire and from now on only firefrozen in fright!

Make a fire, we need some light on the matter, you're totally blinded, have to rely more on your ears, but sounds can catch fire too, and still you give no answer to anything people are asking about, you're composing for the doctor a little silence in advance, you have to give him short breaks, as short as the silent intervals between the projectiles in a burst of machine-gun fire—listen more closely until you hear something, still more closely, until, the sound mounting very softly to your ears, incomprehensible as it makes its way inside your head, you can finally follow those flocks of underground birds before soaring away, swaying, staggering downwards in front of your own self, sliding into the dusk dance of that broken-open autumn evening, through that carousel so prone to pictures inducing dizzy spells, that carousel causing your field of vision to catch fire as it compasses that raging September-evening red in that village there in the Alps, which conceals its huts and houses from itself and those who dwell in them and that keeps itself so hidden among hunching hills, hiding among hills that gather like huge beasts into hill herds and surge over one another in swells and surges, hilloverlapping with their hides, and with their crests hilloverhilling roundabout, overhillhopping hilling themselves, hindhilling hillhollowhill, these just the forehills to other hills, the next hill reaching uphill, breakers at the foot of a mountain, shoreline of a high mountain range —

Doctor Webern is high up in the mountains, you've got to go up there, up to the last story of that huge building there, up to the attic level, and there you must find him, up, up, all the way to the deepest cellar of the sky, all the way up to seventh hell; do you recognize where you are? In the dance hall at Mittersill; all you have to do is take a careful look, out there over the roof, in the air, your room in that largest inn of your village—you're moving like someone who's supposed to be playing the part of a man by the same name as you but who doesn't even know his own name and is conducting himself like a tailor's dummy: quick now, go outside, go down, see how it was in that village in the Alps, where people always have a false idea of their life expectancy, and then keep moving quickly, you don't even have a whole ten years left, all you have are ten minutes, ten seconds after you move on again, gliding through that dark corridor toward the outside of the house, falling into the burning autumn evening as if through a trap door you yourself must open, falling back inward into this postwar time that just goes on enduring —

Faster, Doctor Webern, you have to get down to the valley! Otherwise you'll be late! You need a whole ten years to finally reach the house of your daughter, your son-in-law, where you're invited to dinner, together with your wife—you're looking forward to your first cigar since the war—and you're expecting a late guest besides, one of those gentlemen who remain anonymous while giving a composer what is purportedly his last commission, who pay a good fee in advance but have to pose as themselves the composer of the piece—yes, Doctor Webern, you are certainly going to have to say with special emphasis to this young man later, outside the house, that you're not at all angry with him for those three notes and your . . .

Listen, Raymond, breathe calmly now, just breathe in and then breathe out, and now tell me, are you going to pull the trigger or will someone else pull the trigger now?!—There you are again, you still really don't know anything—Well, that will come out soon enough, who will have fired past the target from where at whom pointing where, because, Raymond, we now make heads with nails, no, nails with heads, and so from now on there simply will not be a single nailed head any more—So all right, breathe in once more and breathe out once more—and soon now don't breathe at all any more, but not just yet, wait for just one single second —

Doctor Webern, please close the door at once! —
No, you're not to go out into the corridor now!
And above all don't step outside the house! —
The cigar?!
Smoke it right here in the room!
No, your wife doesn't mind . . .

in fact, she's glad you're going to . . .
and then, too, you'll now be able to show your grandchildren how
to blow smoke rings when you're smoking a cigar . . .
yes, Doctor Webern, when you now, right away, speaking of this
first cigar—something to celebrate—since the war . . .
Light up, Doctor Webern, set yourself ablaze a bit suddenly . . .
But then that's something else entirely different.

Translator's Afterword

1. Jonke's Comic Vision

Gert Jonke's pattern of developing conflict is fundamentally comic, since his work almost always culminates in harmony achieved or at least imminent by the end of the action. That harmony is deep-seated, never facile. A shallow resolution that does not acknowledge, address, and balance conflict in all its dimensions would only mean glossing over the truth and creating false happy ends. Resolution is hard and honestly won in Jonke, fraught with tensions momentarily governed and reconciled but not banished, gained only after the contending elements have been driven to their polar extremes and then brought to a vibrant center. Jonke's resolutions are often lyrically heightened apotheoses, radiant visions of triumph and peace, but these endings develop organically from the previous tensions, having been earned by negotiating the kinds of dangers and threats comedy can enact and explore more immediately than can tragedy.

Even though comedy, because it promises recognition and resolution before disaster strikes, is equipped to approach potential calamity even more closely than is tragedy—examples from *Lysistrata* through *The Tempest* through *Der Schwierige* to *The Cunning Little Vixen* come to mind at once—it has never been quite respected as a mode of truth. Generalizing about reactions to Hofmannsthal, Richard Alewyn wrote (64) that the somberness of the Protestant work ethic, a prevailing Western mentality still, inclines to judge comedy, especially when manifested through elegance and grace, as frivolous. The somber spirit is not prepared to recognize depth and seriousness where it does not also find pathos and gravity, is disinclined to believe that anything glittering could indeed be gold.

Even though comedy involves far more than slapstick or hilarity, then, a first glance at Jonke's work might make any serious-minded reader nervous, because one strategy in his pushing conflict to extremes is his playful resort to madcap exaggeration. One of his great models is Georg Büchner's comedy *Leonce und Lena*, with its zaniness, its madcap humor, and its sheer beauty of language (Kathrein 7). Jonke is occasionally called a satirist, but the critic who dubbed him a "crafty anarchist of language"

(Reiterer 90) is more accurate. Satire, chastened by irony, underscores order, while parody, based in excess and exaggeration,
unleashes anarchism. Satire enacts a *reductio ad absurdum*,
parody a *multiplicatio ad absurdum*. Jonke portrays an initial
order incrementally undermined by glitches until whole systems
lose coherence and wobble or collapse outright, characters and
settings caught in mayhem that starts small but engulfs the cosmos, growing more hilarious as it grows more chaotic.

Lewis Carroll, Charlie Chaplin, the Marx Brothers, or Jacques
Tati would be right at home in Jonke's world, which often has the
feel of Kafka in slapstick mode. One of his characteristically droll
approaches to autobiography, *Himmelstraße–Erdbrustplatz
oder Das System von Wien*, a personal record named for stops
along streetcar lines in Vienna, purposely debunks the gravity of
most autobiographers from St. Augustine through Jean-Jacques
Rousseau and beyond. Jonke negates the conventional, porten-
tous opening ploy of autobiographies that link such events in nature as comets, constellations, and other signs and wonders to
the birth of the artist. Instead, the chapter about his birth reads
like a lost page from *Tristram Shandy*, if not *Monty Python*, in
its air of clownish mishap, as Jonke relays what he says he was
told: his mother had to search the apartment for her shoes on
that February night and almost didn't make it to the hospital;
when she got there the porter had trouble with his keys and
couldn't open the door at first; the porter, scheduled to go to a
different station, had been about to leave his post anyway; and,
finally, he, the baby, was born blue. Even if all these items are
based in fact, Jonke has arranged them into a poetry of systemic
and increasingly drastic muddle, a coherent vision of an incoherent world making life hard even before birth.

Yet parody and anarchy give way to visionary peace, the wild
struggles in Jonke's works leading to the merited triumph of an
apotheosis, a universal resolution beyond the contingencies of
time and space, as in the four pieces here. Irony contains and
lives with irresolution and disappointment, while anarchy demands some radical solution, surprisingly often a balance emerging out of extremes, so that even the bizarre death of Webern becomes a fitting end, in his own mind, to his musical career. The
autobiographer whose very emergence into the world was
fraught with danger and contingency grows into an astute observer and commentator, a lover of beauty, a man with a mind

and soul capable of finding order and system in humans and their often eccentric, obsessive arrangements, a frail mortal tempted to suicide, buffeted by all the fates and hardships that can beset anyone living between heaven and earth, between the universal *Himmelstraße* and the *Erdbrustplatz* of human striving.

Drawing from the pieces in this volume, the title character in "The Head of George Frederick Handel" ends his life in spiritual ecstacy, seeing himself and his music as a great manifestation of nature in harmonious movement with flocks of birds and flowing rivers, but not until he has suffered more than once the pain and fear of physical collapse and the loneliness of artistic isolation and rejection. Far from delaying or muting the sense of glory at the end, those sufferings are essential to its attainment. In *Blinding Moment*, Anton Webern gains the strength and vision to conduct Gustav Mahler's monumental symphonies by walking along the beach and recognizing Mahler's rhythmic patterns in the pounding of the surf; after Mahler's death, Webern finds through these walks on the beach the power to teach their parts, one by one, to each individual member of the workers' chorus assigned to perform Mahler's Symphony Number 8 ("Symphony of a Thousand"), since none of them could read music, a feat so arduous that it would not be considered possible if it were not documented as fact. Yet this was the same conductor who could not get past the first few measures of Alban Berg's Violin Concerto in rehearsals for its premiere in Barcelona in 1936; he was so paralyzed by grief that he could not proceed. Webern's life operates as a system of achievement alternating between superhuman skill and frustrating paralysis, and it is resolved in a freakish and violent way, but one he accepts as the last logical phase of his artistic development. Ludwig van Beethoven is flooded with light from his own music at the radiant end of *Gentle Rage or The Ear Machinist*. As the last movement of the *Hammerklavier* sonata, Opus 106, sounds autonomously from the piano, the brilliance of the light becomes gradually more intense. But this godlike creator whose work generates light is also the suffering mortal who undergoes isolation and acute depression about his deafness and who can explode in fierce, ugly bursts of temper when he feels threatened. His final serenity balances the opposing forces of his personality but does not dispel them.

The kind of comic resolution that Jonke's characters often achieve originates at the source, in the order of nature. As already noted, Handel gains energy from birds in flight, from rivers in motion, from water surging up from the earth at the hot springs, Webern finds artistic meaning and personal strength in the surging breakers of the sea, and Beethoven basks as man and artist in brilliant light, his eyes often doing the work of his ears. Comedy culminates in growth, renewal, and the greening of the land, internalizes into character the kind of fertility that can come only from nature's balance of cycles like light and dark, hot and cold, the seasons, the tides, perpetual waxing and waning, growing and dying. Between heaven and earth is eternal recurrence in time, as the birds point out with alternating solemnity and buffoonery in "Catalogue d'oiseaux," Jonke's tribute to Olivier Messiaen, so the doom of mortality gives way to the certainty of rebirth outside of time. The connection of human consciousness to natural cycles enables renewal and hope.

Balance also depends on a living connection of the self to its individual nature as well, especially to a sense of what the person needs to gain fulfillment. Jonke's work divides quite evenly between characters who suffer but triumph because they have pursued in the face of persecution and failure what they knew they were called to do and those who grow paralyzed and shut down because they have persisted in feeding their egos, perpetuating illusions, and following wrong directions in their lives; the four pieces here offer instances of positive psychological development, while the novellas *gegenwart der erinnerung* (memory at present) and *gradus ad parnassum*, collected in the volume *Schule der Geläufigkeit* (The School for Velocity, after Carl Czerny), trace the ruin of characters who grow more delusional and destructive the more they persist in arbitrary courses of action unrelated to their needs or natures.

This essential need to lead a fulfilled life by finding and pursuing one's true direction marks Jonke's own development as a writer, so much so that some biographical background would be a pertinent illustration of patterns in his work. Strong determination to pursue his calling shaped his life, just as his characters become authentic only when they follow what they find to be their natural course. Jonke was born in Klagenfurt, the capital city of Carinthia, in 1946. His father showed almost no interest in him or his mother (Lux 48). In those days, the head of the municipal family services department was automatically appointed legal guardian of all children born to single mothers (Jonke "Individuum und Metamorphose" in *Stoffgewitter* 14-5), and that arrangement was to have a major unintended impact on Jonke's literary development by setting up a strengthening resistance. His place of birth is itself notable, since Klagenfurt has produced a markedly high proportion of gifted Austrian authors—Ingeborg Bachmann, Peter Handke, and Werner Kofler are only the most prominent. As with the Southern Renaissance in American literature, it is almost as if provincial restrictiveness, lock-step social traditionalism, reactionary politics (Klagenfurt is the bastion of Jörg Haider's Nazi-friendly, jingoistic Freedom Party), marginalization or exclusion of minorities (Slovenes in Carinthia), and hostility to any cosmopolitan outlook provided the energizing alienation needed for writers to find their voices (see Amann "Literaturlandschaft Kärnten" 205-08).

Jonke notes that Bachmann called Klagenfurt "a good city to get away from" (Jonke *Stoffgewitter* 12), a judgment borne out by the early departure of practically every gifted writer, himself included. He was bored in school, mediocre at best. "They once denied people schooling; today what they teach them is how to act with as little imagination as possible," he said to Harald Friedl (106). Yet it was a poem by Georg Trakl—"Sommersneige" ("The Remains of Summer")—copied onto the board by a teacher that made him decide against a career in music and that led to his "taking up residence in language and living in rooms of narration" as he puts it (Jonke *Stoffgewitter* 7). No less bowled over by the beauty of Trakl's poem than happy to discover that poetry doesn't have to rhyme (Friedl 98), Jonke began writing and publishing his own poems in the Klagenfurt journal of experimental literature, *Der Bogen*, at age sixteen, under the spell of Trakl and reinforced by his encounters with Giuseppe Ungaretti and other Italian "Hermeticists." At this point, his legal guardian stepped in, disturbed by Jonke's pursuing "such nonsense" when his grades were low. He pressured the editor into refusing further submissions and forbade Jonke to continue publishing. "This man even had the audacity to threaten me with reform school" (Jonke *Stoffgewitter* 14-5). His discovering and being included a few years later in a group of like-minded experimental writers in Graz, the newly-formed Grazer Autorenversammlung (Graz Authors' Assembly), gave him a structure earlier denied him.

The guardian kept a firm grip, meanwhile, demanding that Jonke fulfill his compulsory military service immediately after graduation (Lux 49). Predictably, this approach backfired, and in two main ways that only fixed Jonke's course all the more unerringly. First, Jonke developed "an extremely troubled relationship with bureaucracy of every kind" and an "allergic reaction to supervision, organization, and the largely prevailing politics of administration by pigeon-holing" (Jonke *Stoffgewitter* 15), which he sublimated into a critical position that inheres in his very manner of literary composition. "My rage is great, though not usually directed at any given object," Jonke told Harald Friedl (99), confessing that as an exception he had Ronald Reagan in mind when describing the "President of the New World" in his novel *Erwachen zum großen Schlafkrieg* (1982). The radiance of the president's fake grin causes his face to burst into flames.

The other outcome of these efforts to thwart Jonke's writing was to strengthen his determination by making it clear that his survival required absolute independence and focus on his art. Combined with a modest, gentle manner that seems almost at odds with his fierce concentration, that independence has given him the resolve to explore his experimental artistic processes with serenity. Jonke gets along unusually well with almost all his fellow writers and enjoys their company (Friedl 112), he readily grants interviews and gives readings, and he is duly eager for his work to become better known. Even so, to quote one of his most astute readers, he "tenaciously pursues his artistic research work from book to book, totally unimpressed and uninfluenced by anything called success or literary wheeling and dealing" (Amann "Des Unsagbaren Nachtgesang" 52). Another observer (Russegger in Lux 61) recalls Jonke's characteristic behavior at the twentieth-anniversary celebration of the Ingeborg Bachmann Prize in 1996:

> While TV people, politicians and cultural officials, actors and writers, all bursting with high self-estimates, talked all about themselves and their insights on Ingeborg Bachmann, this artist sat under the fierce glare of the lights and held a monologue . . . in part reading from his manuscript . . . in part extemporizing, that blazed with poetic flashes of intellectual lightning.

Jonke enrolled at the University of Vienna in 1966, purportedly for courses in history, philosophy, musicology, and German literature, but he soon grew even more dissatisfied with higher education than with his earlier schooling, finding most of the professors bored, uninvolved, authoritarian, and trapped in routine. He looked back on his formal studies–or lack thereof–as "a colossal fraud: . . . on my part, a fraud against scholarship, because I thought I could attain it, and a fraud by scholarship against me, because it made me think I was indispensable to it" (Jonke *Himmelstraße* 43-5). He was more interested in the work he was pursuing in the School of Film, Television, and Theater Directing at the Academy for Music and the Performing Arts, but he kept enrolling at the university, too–there were no fees then–because his student housing was very inexpensive, and he had to be registered to keep it (Lux 51).

What Jonke was really doing all that time was writing, mainly a novel called *Das System von Wien*, never completed in that form but variously reworked later. From his first publication on, *Geometrischer Heimatroman* (1969) (*Geometric Regional Novel*, trans. Johannes W. Vazulik), he has enjoyed persistent and widespread acclaim. No less eminent a contemporary than Peter Handke reviewed *Geometrischer Heimatroman* very favorably in no less eminent a publication than the German weekly *Der Spiegel* (Handke 251-5). Jonke was the inaugural winner of the coveted Ingeborg Bachmann Prize in 1977, and he has repeatedly been honored since, most recently by the Major Austrian State Prize for Literature and the Nestroy Prize for an outstanding play, to name only two of many. He is constantly traveling through Germany, Austria, and German-speaking Switzerland for performances and readings. His life has by no means been idyllic, however, for Jonke has had to negotiate the same polarities that belong to any life honestly lived. An infant son died, he has suffered physical impairment and mental collapse, and he had a long period of dependency on alcohol (Jonke *Stoffgewitter* 76-7), but his persistence in his calling has lent him the same simplicity and singleness of purpose that mark the strivings of Beethoven, Handel, Webern, and other protagonists in his work.

The quest for balance with opposites, that hallmark of comedy, also has a political dimension especially pertinent to any Austrian writer. Jonke's typical pattern of driving opposite forces to extremes can be understood as a kind of artistic response to or

even a critical engagement with the constant smoothing over of
conflict at the heart of Austrian public life still today. Robert Menasse (27) is only one of many commentators to point out that
avoidance of extremes, eagerness to compromise, and quick
searches for consensus at almost any cost have characterized the
social and political arrangements of the Second Austrian Republic since its proclamation in 1955, largely because contending political parties, complete with private militias, earlier destroyed
the First Republic by their growing intransigence, mutual dis-
trust, and refusal to give ground, creating a climate of both paralysis and violence leading to an impasse in which Parliament
was eventually annulled and a clerical-fascist dictatorship pro-
claimed in 1933. After 1945, then, with full public approval, real
decision-making was quietly removed from official channels,
taken out of the hands of the parties and their legislative bodies
and turned over to organizations like labor unions, chambers of
commerce, associations of managers and owners, meeting to
reach compromise behind closed doors, beyond the destructive
"bickering" of the parties and the "nit-picking" of legislators. The
great advantage of the harmony since 1945 is its workability.
Strikes and other confrontations are almost unknown in an
economy that has grown steadily more prosperous for the last
sixty years, and the Austrian population at large still strongly endorses the harmony that results. Open processes are likely to be
distrusted as radical or subject to demagoguery, by contrast.

Menasse argues that the harmony emerging from this system
is a sham, whatever its advantages (27). Because that system can
be validated in a constitutional state only if the pretense is up-
held that compromises are being reached openly and democrati-
cally, with ample public participation, there is no actual way of
addressing the real dynamic or even finding out much in particular about its workings. The very efficacy of the system depends
on its not being scrutinized; as long as the legislature goes
through the motions of passing the right laws, no one need call
things by their right name. Worse yet, the Austrian system of
"social partnership" approaches all compromises as if they were
proof that no conflict ever existed in the first place, whereas any
compromise is a temporarily successful negotiation between
competing interests, with necessarily recurring conflict at its
core. What would there be to compromise about otherwise? As
Menasse notes (27), no society can hope to be "harmonious" in

the dangerously simplistic sense that Austria claims to be, but the social partnership is famous for insuring that a compromise will result–whatever the issue–before the problem even comes up for discussion.

So far, so enviable, but what pertains to an individual pertains to a whole society. The price of shallow harmony is fundamental refusal to face tensions, problems, and unresolved issues on any level, to violate truth by pretending there is nothing negative to discuss. Individual character can never develop under such circumstances; nor can a nation deal with its history if it pretends that there was never anything wrong. Austria's literal moment of truth came very belatedly, during the campaign for the presidency of the republic in 1986, when Kurt Waldheim hedged, stonewalled, and lost his memory about possible Nazi party membership and assignment during World War II to an SS unit. Even when confronted with pictures of himself in uniform, he let his handlers do the talking, and they finally persuaded him to make a statement that tore the country apart: "I only did my duty," a polarizing justification that finally brought the entire Austrian relation to Nazism out into the open. This forty-years belated confrontation with the past was the very first occasion on which any public mechanism emerged that would allow the topic of Austria's Nazi past, always typically ignored or smoothed over before, even to be broached at large. Fiction writers, poets, historians, psychologists and others who had addressed the topic before 1986 were deeply respected by a few but often marginalized and maligned as "foulers of their own nests." Life was not made easy for Gerhard Fritsch, Friedrich Heer, Marie-Thérèse Kerschbaumer, Hans Lebert, Helmut Qualtinger, Erika Weinzierl, and other writers who engaged with a past few wanted to face.

This political background helps illustrate the typical intransigence, stubbornness, and fierce determination of Jonke's characters. Rather than temporize, deny, or compromise their truth, they will starve, make enemies, or live in exile to pursue their art. It is not very "Austrian" of Beethoven to explode in fury at Schindler and throw him out after a ferocious tirade, but the outburst comes at a moment when Beethoven feels Schindler attempting to curtail his art, to deny it expression, and to call his creativity itself into question. Beethoven has no choice at that point, for he would turn into the mentally ill incompetent Schindler considers him if he did not handle the matter as he does. His very identity is at stake. That is also why he takes an extreme individualistic position on the subject of natural rights, rejecting compromise and refusing to grant that society has any right to curtail his activities on the basis of imaginary obligations on his part. Likewise, Alexander von Zemlinsky is baffled at Webern's determination to return immediately to Vienna, where he has no work and no prospects, before his furniture is even moved into his new apartment in Prague. Webern explains over and over that he is sure he will not be able to compose at all if he becomes caught up in the attractive musical opportunities offered by his new conducting position in Prague, so he would rather forfeit income, security, friendship, and community than jeopardize his calling. It bothers him not at all that Zemlinsky appears to consider him insane, or, if it does, Zemlinksy's view does not budge his utter determination to pursue his craft on his terms, ultimately finding violent death to be a logical fulfillment of his work as a composer, whereas conducting *Parsifal* in Prague would have been a hindrance to his real task. Severe strokes with paralysis, the closing of the theaters, abandonment by fickle audiences, mockery by his rival John Gay, his dubious status as a deserter from his position at the court of Hannover, the seeming loss of his talent and inspiration—none of these crippling forces can do any more than stop Handel temporarily. Like Beethoven and Webern, he is sustained by a kind of sacred rage, having scorned the "sensible" advice of a physician who considers recovery impossible. Casting aside the doctor's warnings about overdoing it, he uncompromisingly follows his own treatment program at the spa, energized by waters flowing from the very center of the earth to the point where he can improvise at the organ with greater virtuosity and more profound musicianship than ever. All his setbacks have in fact prepared him for the supreme moment of receptivity when he first encounters the text of *Messiah* and finds his life's full redemption in setting it feverishly, in a burst of inspiration he considers divine and that brings about his own rebirth and renewal.

2. Jonke's Musical Modality

It would be hard to think of any country whose writers exhibit a higher concentration of musicianship than Austria. To pick almost random examples from the twentieth century, Elfriede Jelinek and Thomas Bernhard had extensive conservatory training. Jelinek's novel *Die Klavierspielerin* (*The Piano Player*), famous outside Austria in its filmed version, shows detailed understanding from the professional standpoint of practice technique and repertoire development. Bernhard's play *Die Macht der Gewohnheit* (Force of Habit) presents a group of people who have been rehearsing Schubert's "Trout" Quintet for twenty-two years without getting very far, and his novel *Der Untergeher* (*The Loser*) displays the kind of minute familiarity with conservatory routine that could only arise from direct experience. H. C. Artmann was a singer and a virtuoso on several folk instruments. Ernst Jandl was an expert on jazz and an occasional performer. Gerhard Rühm is a pianist as well as a dramatist and poet. Hans Lebert was both a Wagnerian tenor and a novelist whose fiction develops on the structural principle of the *Leitmotiv*. Heimito von Doderer was a cellist of almost professional competence; he developed extensive musical structures in literary works to which he gave titles like "Divertimento," "Sonatina," and "Variations," culminating in a huge project he did not live to complete, a tetralogy called *Novel No. 7* in homage to Beethoven's Seventh Symphony, with one novel for each movement.

Even with such comparisons, Jonke might well be the most musical of all Austrian writers. He remembers his mother as a fine pianist, barred from a career only because her nerves could not stand the strain and excitement of concertizing. She would have had to be very proficient technically even to attempt Ravel's *Jeux d'eau*, the piece her five-year-old demanded she play him every night before bedtime. "It enchanted me," he recalls, adding that "my fanatical love of music has stayed with me. I don't think I could live without music" (Kathrein 7). Jonke intended to become a pianist himself, and he studied for some years at the conservatory in Graz, stopping when he decided in his teens to devote himself to writing. Not only was he "too lazy to practise," as he told Kathrein (7), but he came to a realistic awareness that he lacked the required talent and dedication to achieve a level with which he would be satisfied. That poem by Trakl on the blackboard thus brought Jonke's piano study to a quick end, as a new world of poetry opened to him, a poetry aspiring to the condition of music, in Walter Pater's phrase. In his essay "Die Überschallgeschwindigkeit der Musik" (*Stoffgewitter* 80-93), on musical performance, Jonke rejects as too dogmatic Nietzsche's contention in *The Birth of Tragedy* that language can approximate but never capture the innermost soul of music (89). He notes instead that literature, the art of the word, has been used with great success in the twentieth century to produce poems that have the full impact of music, in which pure sound plays as important a structural role as do the meanings of the words. Music functions by turns as allusion, plot, metaphor, method, and structure in his work, underlying every aspect of Jonke's creativity to such an extent that he has at times referred to himself more as a composer than as a writer in any ordinary sense (Friedl 101). Although he would no longer describe himself in that way (Kling Interview 2004), his work may still be more thoroughly governed by his lifelong involvement with music than that of almost any other writer.

It was no surprise, then, to encounter Jonke as a guest of honor and a participant in the opening round-table discussion during the festival of Anton Webern's music at the Konzerthaus in Vienna on June 5 and 6, 2004 (detailed in Lasinger 3), since his film script and novella *Geblendeter Augenblick* (*Blinding Moment*) take the bizarre accidental shooting of Webern as their starting point, but he was additionally present, unlike the other guests, at every performance throughout two full days, rapt with admiration and enthusiastic about sharing his views, which reveal part of his own artistic intent and practise without his ever mentioning his work unless asked specifically about it. Jonke commented on the brevity of Webern's music, not as a quality in itself but as the mark of a transparent intricacy Webern achieved by organizing every last element of an extremely elaborate but logical world of sound into a space so compressed that the listener can apprehend the structure only by paying unusually close attention on more than one hearing. Every tiny element indispensable to the edifice, every piece amazingly short, but yet containing whole worlds for us to seek out and explore: that was the essence of Jonke's remarks on Webern (Kling Interview 2004), and while Jonke's art tends toward expansion rather than compression, he shares with Webern the command of highly complex form by strategically ingenious deployment of every small component.

Jonke's essays on music are unsurpassed for lucid erudition and profound empathy, ranging with great originality over areas of discourse not usually connected and filled with exactly the

kind of scholarly knowledge and competence he says he could
never have attained. Examples are "Die Überschallgeschwindigkeit der Musik" (*Stoffgewitter* 80-93), on musical performance, "Ein anderes Kärnterlied" (*Stoffgewitter* 62-72), about–
among other things–the role Carinthian folk tunes have played
in suggesting themes to various composers who spent time there,
like Johannes Brahms and Gustav Mahler, and "Verheimlichte
Kontinente" (*Stoffgewitter* 73-9), a brilliant appreciation of Alban Berg. These are sovereign, independent essays in themselves, and the last two function "musically" in turn as preludes
in the discursive mode to the literary piece that follows them, the
Webern novella *Blinding Moment* (94-159).

   Jonke was encouraged to write more about specifically musical subjects and personalities after the success of his *Schule der
Geläufigkeit*, a paired set of novellas about artists, especially
about a composer and a performer who have come to grief. As he
turned increasingly to the topic, incorporting imaginary and real
composers into his work, he became aware that his identity as an
imaginative artist was threatened by requests to write more or
less standard biographies of composers, studies of the life-and-
works variety. As a result, he saw to it that every work he produced, in whatever genre, would answer first the call of imaginative structure, which is not to observe chronology or furnish critical assessment but to allow forms to emerge in congruity with
the demands of content. Even though Jonke modestly states that
his musical knowledge comes only from standard reference
works, his command is in fact encyclopedic, and virtually any
reference to events in the lives of the composers depicted here–
Handel's keyboard duel with Domenico Scarlatti, Webern's reputation as a Nazi, Beethoven's obsessive concern to find gadgets
that might restore his hearing–is firmly grounded in documented
fact upon which Jonke then weaves his invention. To repeat,
though, Jonke is an artist, so he always transforms the ascertainable facts into a literary structure arising from the nature of the
main character's conflict. Especially through the device of governing time by rearranging it out of chronological sequence to illustrate the cyclical recurrence of struggles in the composer's life,
Jonke avoids the platitudes built into so many films and fictional
treatments of artists' lives that never free themselves imagina-
tively from the imperatives of biographical reporting and thus
fail as works of art. Jonke always folds the biographical elements

into an autonomous literary structure with its own internally generated laws. Composing in every form, Jonke repeatedly turns to music and musicians as analogues for the process of shaping form from sound, of governing chaos through artistic structure.

Allusions to musical works and adaptations of musical forms are ubiquitous in Jonke's fiction, even in works that do not have music as their subject. Jonke mentioned to Friedl (105) that he instinctively draws on "sonata form, fugue form, rondo form, variation form, passacaglia form," not as purposely applied principles of composition but simply from being so saturated with musical structures that they emerge on their own with no set intent on his part. *Geometric Regional Novel*, for instance, draws on rondo-variation form, which alternates a relatively simple theme (A) with progressively more elaborate variations developing from that theme; the overall structure is A–B–A–C–A–D–A–E, and so on. (Among many possible instances, two great arias by Mozart are especially clear textbook examples of rondo-variation form, Fiordiligi's "Per pietà, ben mio, perdona" from Act II of *Così fan tutte* and Vitellia's "Non più di fiori" from Act II of *La clemenza di Tito*.) Jonke's theme, the (A) in *Geometric Regional Novel*, is represented by the chapters entitled "The Village Square," which always begin with the same brief exchange between two people debating how to cross the empty village square without being detected. That theme creates a clearly discernible and literal point of departure for progressively more extended, complex, and wide-ranging variations, each of which moves geographically ever farther from the square to encompass more and more of the surroundings while incorporating more and more of the deeper history and wider organization of the village. The unifying structural movement of *Geometric Regional Novel* enacts the spread of political tyranny as the variations in their increasing complexity and wider geographical range model the growing encroachment of authoritarianism through greater control of seemingly harmless, traditional social arrangements meant to uphold good order. The vehicle for that structural movement is the simple theme, the verbal exchange at the start of alternate chapters, beginning with the first, in which readers can already detect a vague, pervasive apprehension or even muted fear of a paternalistic authority that eventually engulfs everything.

Seen as adaptations of musical forms to prose, devices of style that may appear simply tics or idiosyncrasies on Jonke's part, indulgences in verbal acrobatics with no specific grounding or particular function, actually reveal themselves as efficient strategies in the mode of art, which achieves its communication–like all literature, and even more like music itself–through formal structure, not through discursive categories. In a short piece like "Danube River Bridge," for example, several phrases recur notably more often than is needed simply to establish meaning; the main two are the variants on being "absolutely certain to this day" and the frequent mention of the Danube emptying into the Black Sea. Not advancing "story" as such, they yet perform a vital function as lexical groups marking the shape of what are equivalent in words to four-bar and eight-bar phrases of a melody, whose trajectory depends for structural coherence on the refrain-like recurrence of like units, on repetition, with variety, of similar intervals and rhythms. Such an organizing technique becomes unmistakably clear on hearing aloud a story like "Danube River Bridge" or any other short piece, in which the rhythmic repetitions of words, the bar lines, if one will, work as another form of punctuation to indicate units of speech. Jonke is in this respect similar to other novelists–Henry James, James Joyce, William Faulkner, Samuel Beckett–whose alleged sytlistic complexities of syntax and sentence form reveal the greatest lucidity of structure as soon as the works are read out aloud.

That device of melodic-like development by phrasal repetition is only one example of an observation Gamper has made (160-1) about Jonke's work as a whole–the strictness of the musical form constitutes a necessary counterbalance to the ever-present "Aberwitz," the zaniness, lunacy, and extreme whimsy, disciplining the imminent threat of chaos by containing it within a disciplined shape. Another such prominent verbal hallmark drawn from musical form is the frequent proliferation of language in the manner of a cadenza, a virtuosic elaboration of the basic structural material to display the skill of composer and performer and to cap the thematic logic, such as we find in the relentless cascades of synonyms in the pages-long list of guidelines, mainly prohibitions, of course, given to the schoolchildren in *Geometric Regional Novel* (43-6).

3. Four Musical Pieces

The title of the story Jonke published in 1988, *The Head of George Frederick Handel*, deflects at once any expectation of standard biography, documentation, or chronology by pointing directly to the form of interior monologue. Invoking works like Hermann Broch's *The Death of Virgil*, in which the dying hours of an artist's life are passed in review, *The Head of George Frederick Handel* captures the composer's thoughts and memories during his last eighteen hours, but Handel dies humanly fulfilled and pantheistically transformed into an enduring force of nature's beauty, as opposed to the doubt and fear tormenting Virgil. There may be an element of political or social comment in the contrast, for the narrator emphasizes that Handel had worked free of royal and aristocratic patronage and was able to make a living on his own resources. Even during the time of his dependence on aristocratic patrons, he had found ways of being treated as a social equal, not condescended to as an upper-level servant but received as a gentleman. By contrast, Virgil is tormenting himself on his deathbed for having been the almost too compliant court poet, remaining the dependent imperial functionary by abetting the power of Augustus Caesar through work that elevates the emperor's conquests and victories to mythic status and epic scope. While Handel had quietly but rebelliously removed himself from his court position at Hannover, with no authorization to stay away, Virgil worries that he never transcended the imperial power structure of which the *Aeneid* is an unqualified endorsement. At any rate, Jonke needed to be especially careful to make Handel's dying happiness psychologically convincing, since his source for the story was a work that had reached its optimistic ending with somewhat facile assurance.

Opportunities for working in television film, a subgenre of performing art in which he had been trained, opened up to Jonke in 1979, and in a way that seems to come straight out of a story by him. Perhaps only he would also have seized on the chance to reshape the two TV scripts he wrote in the 1980s and later turn them into fictional works. (The second is *Blinding Moment*, the novella version of which included in this volume and discussed later in this afterword.) Jonke had been writing stage and radio plays for a number of years when he unexpectedly received a pleading phone call from Frankfurt in 1979. A producer at Hessische Rundfunk (Hessian Radio and Television) told him that the station had on its hands a completed film, directed by Klaus Lindemann and edited into final form, about the last hours in the life of Handel, but that the script was a disaster in spite of being adapted from a renowned quasi-fictional essay by Stefan Zweig titled "Georg Friedrich Händels Auferstehung" (Zweig 73-100), one of the studies in his beloved and once famous collection of historical miniatures called *Sternstunden der Menschheit* (translated into English as *The Tide of Fortune*) (Kling Interview 2004; Schmidt-Dengler 325). The script was so unworkable that the director had decided to abandon the project unless Jonke was willing to attempt a total rewrite, but under the odd constraint that the timing of any new script would have to match the film exactly as it stood, since there was no opportunity for further shooting or recutting. The unusual nature of the challenge appealed to Jonke, and the result, *Händels Auferstehung* (1980), was very favorably received, so much so that his successful rescue operation would lead to the commission for *Blinding Moment*.

Jonke's approach in both the script and the story eliminates a dated tone of confidence in cultural progress, an "onward-and-upward" view of history that characterizes much of Zweig's non-fiction (or semi-fiction) and that today seems naïve and at times even histrionic, to the point of marring some of his otherwise excellent biographies and historical studies. Jonke denies glib progressive views of linear history by incorporating backward movement through time and by layering recurrences of the same patterns in Handel's life at different periods. It is an instructive study in the changing nature of artistic form to read Zweig's piece, with its mainly linear and chronological structure, and then to read Jonke and see how he transformed large stretches of the same material into a cyclical narration that achieves release from time. Schmidt-Dengler (325) taxes Zweig with "an occasionally superficial relation of history and art," noting too that Jonke, by choosing the interior monologue, brings "calculated distance" to the material as opposed to Zweig's "overheated" emotionalism, because interior monologue prevents imposing authorial value systems or judgments. Jonke had learned well from earlier fictional works to stay free of all authorial intrusion and let the material develop structurally on its own terms.

Jonke's long short story or short novella–thirty-one printed pages in the first edition–narrated from within Handel's mind but in third person, begins with the composer's memory of per-

forming the *Royal Fireworks Music* in 1748 and leaps directly to
the last hours of Handel's life in April of 1759, with constant
shuttling back and forth in time. Handel has been felled by a
massive stroke, as a result of which disorientation the gigantic
fireworks display celebrating the Peace of Aachen becomes con-
flated in his mind with traditional bonfires announcing spring
and with passing allusions to the burning bush of Exodus and the
flame of the Paschal candle. In fact, Jonke consistently depicts
the sources of Handel's creative power as a compound of the ancient four elements of earth, air, fire, and water. Some combination of them is always in play whenever Handel experiences a rebirth or healing that releases his musicianship anew. Rain and
snow cause new growth by washing away at the end of winter the
ash from the previous year's fires. The movement of the birds
traces the patterns of the winds in which Handel hears music
while others hear only random noise. The primal source of Handel's musical art is truly cosmic, arising in the fire of the stars, in
". . . the primordial sound made by the splattering of a sun so distant and alien as to be conceivable by no one, as if the shadow of
the noise made by its gradual extinguishing through many millions of years of growing dusk and twilight had wended its way
behind his brow." The waters rising up from the core of the earth
and purified by coursing through layers of rock wash away his
paralysis and restore motion. Only those removed from the re-
newing processes of nature—here the narcissistic and greedy castrati, eager to profit from their loss—appear psychically paralyzed, intent only on their own advantage and uninterested in
humanization.

As Handel submits to the processes of nature, allowing them
to shape him, so nature grants reciprocity. It becomes his power
and privilege, after a period of estrangement, to shape nature in
turn, to govern and articulate it through form, which is the activity of any artist. "He ordained the flow of water music on the
Thames, that the river subordinate itself to his rhythms . . . that
its waves beat in a dance to the exact measure of his pipes and
reeds . . . ." Indicatively for the political aspect of the story,
Handel's aim in governing the river through his *Water Music* is
to placate the king, the sovereign who has become his ruler by
ascending the throne of England but also the same Duke of Hannover from whom he had absented himself without permission.
Yet there is no thought of imposition on the forces of nature

through political power. Instead, Handel has been granted dominion over the Thames by submitting with joy and humility to
nature's rhythms, not by any exercise of rule or might derived
only from human contrivance.

Handel recalls on his deathbed that the same kind of soaring
or floating sensation had come over him once before, intensify-
ing his creative powers when it passed, though it had meant living for four months in the left side of his body only. Now he
knows, though, that this new episode of "floating above his own
body" and witnessing with eye and ear a "transparent reflector of
sounds never heard before" has struck with determined finality
as he approaches for the last time the great fire, the mighty wind,
the surging waters, the solid earth. He feels completed, fulfilled
in his calling. "He loved the work [*Messiah*], because he sensed
himself to have been created, formed entirely anew, along with
it." Lux writes (59) that "Handel is unlike so many of the artists,
impaired and merely running in place, who people Jonke's
world; he is an ideal." We could add that part of his ideal status
arises from his having come as close to achieving his own ideal as
he could and therefore senses his link to the nature into which he
is dissolving as he thinks of his own soul while observing flocks
of birds moving "through the opened cataracts of the sky." That
is in essence the movement of all four pieces in this collection.

Religious imagery and language suffuse *The Head of George
Frederick Handel*, as they do in so many of Jonke's works, and
they are appropriate here for thoughts filling the mind of an artist, one whose creative work is always an attempt to reenact *logos*, to make the word so compelling that it becomes the deed, as
in God's original work of creation (see Zweig 87). Instead of re-
vealing the misplaced pride and the arrogation to themselves of
God's functions that marked the artists in *Schule der Geläufigkeit*, however, Handel's religious allusions here perform the opposite function of deepening his joy at reaching the converging
point of music and the Godhead, at resolving his individual self
into an ineffable state in which his music is one segment of an
entire cosmos of light and sound.

Even though Jonke occasionally takes passages of exact word-
ing directly from Zweig, he adds an element to his source that
suggests a covert autobiographical intent, removing the last
hours of Handel's life even further from the standard life-and-
works approach to the composer. As Handel recalls patrons and

enemies, friends and foes, triumphs and setbacks, he dwells especially on John Gay, whose ballad-opera farce *The Beggar's
Opera* (1728) mocked all the lofty conventions, the deities and
the machinery, the exceptional musical complexity and virtuosity, the regal and splendid effects of Handel's ornate Italian operas with their bravura display, virtuosity, and sublimity. The dying Handel is too close to finality to be petty, but he admits that
the sympathy he feels for the passing of Gay's vogue is a "grieving
tinged with malice." Splendidly self-confident in his last moments, Handel clearly views the crude, parodistic effects of *The
Beggar's Opera*, bidding for popularity by challenging and offering a satiric popular alternative to the more ornate Italian art, as
beneath contempt, unfit to be mentioned in the same breath with
his own demanding, immensely refined works, offered in the
form of oratorios after the fad for Italian opera had passed, but
themselves as unregenerately recondite and sophisticated as the
actual operas.

There is no reference at all to Gay and *The Beggar's Opera*
anywhere in Zweig, so Jonke's inclusion of that contrast to Handel's art is the point at which one can recognize Jonke's engagement with his own aesthetic concerns, as Schmidt-Dengler argues (325). Sure of his artistic process, unwilling ever to con-
demn another artist, Jonke can yet be seen as presenting in "The
Head of George Frederick Handel" a spirited vindication of his
own rarified and highly mannered work, an *apologia* as a writer
who could never be popular because his arcane art is incompati-
ble with crowd-pleasing. In his masque *Acis and Galatea*, Handel stylizes his own suffering and loss, but also his triumph over
them through art, through governed order and elegant balance.
Jonke seems in turn to be writing his own processes of elaboration, recondite reference, demanding style, and uncompromising
complexity into the highly convoluted single sentence, with
clauses intricately folded into one another, that describes and
encompasses the whole world of the masque it is about, with its
polarities from violence and loss to fulfillment and reconcilia-
tion. Likewise, the magical transformation of one stylized human
artifact into another through the force of art, as when the cathedral turns into a ship through Handel's improvisation at the organ, testifies to Jonke's view that the structures and shapes of art
have sovereign power to change hearts and minds, literally to
move lives as Handel is transported across the English Channel

and back to London. It is no mere metaphor to say that a person engrossed in a work of art is in "transports," and Jonke makes that state become literal in this story and other works.

Handel is indeed so transcendently serene and focused, so elevated in his view of approaching eternity, that the language of his story is even more exalted and rhapsodic than usual for Jonke. Schmidt-Dengler sees it as characterized by a "solemnity behind which an apotheosis of art can be seen but which nonetheless at times threatens to topple over into parody" (325). Certainly *The Head of George Frederick Handel* is the most serious and compelling treatment of art Jonke had written up to that point, a work mostly free of his usual overt clowning and hilarity and perhaps not quite typical for that reason. At any rate, readers can only marvel at the imaginative triumph of transmuting more or less standard biography into a dazzling monologue of Handel's last moments as woven around the facts of his life. The highly poetic imagery is entirely plausible as Handel enters into a state of pantheistic wonder at the way in which his own music has come ever closer to that of the spheres. His farewell appearance conducting *Messiah* reveals a serenity, a oneness with nature, and a total human fulfillment that make Handel godlike but that could only have emerged from his many trials. He could have remained successful by conforming to the fashions of the moment, by settling for the simpering, shallow, denatured Arcadianism so prevalent in his earlier years and so memorably invoked in the scene of the cardinal's garden party, but to the almost excessive elegance and polish of Arcadian and pastoral conventions, in which he outdid all his contemporaries, he added the uncompromising truth of profound self-expression even when thwarted, even when "despisèd and rejected," to use a phrase from Isaiah as cited in *Messiah*. Jonke implies that Handel is in part writing about himself when setting those words from Isaiah about the Suffering Servant, but he handles the matter with his usual distance and reticence, as opposed to a ponderously sentimental moment in Zweig (83), when Handel, feeling alone and abandoned, explicitly uses the words of Christ on the cross, "My God, my God, why hast Thou forsaken me?" Less is more; Jonke incorporates the moment in Zweig (86) when Handel, looking at the text of *Messiah* for the first time, construes the opening words, "Comfort ye," as being about himself and addressed to him individually through Providence, and he lets it go at that, allowing a network of implication to arise from that one moment. The effect is to make the triumph, the apotheosis of Handel at the end even more convincing by not underscoring the obvious.

Of the four pieces in this collection, the one least likely to be mistaken for a standard biography is "Catalogue d'oiseaux," since the composer to whom it is a tribute, Olivier Messiaen, does not appear. Instead of incorporating the person of the composer, as in the other three works, "Catalogue d'oiseaux," first published in 2002 in *kolik*, a Viennese journal of experimental writing, is an homage to Messiaen's gigantic three-hour piano work of the same title from 1958. The title in turn recalls the Homeric device of placing extensive catalogues at intervals in epic poems. But if the term "catalogue" suggests in turn that only one of the humbler epic devices, a simple itemization by category, is being requisitioned, the range and scope Messiaen's and Jonke's works reveal them as full epics, containing whole physical and spiritual worlds in their closed systems. This attempt to evoke universality by cataloguing is what helps that device further an epic, in fact. After Homer has listed all the ships waiting in the harbor, there is probably nothing more to learn about seafaring, and it is seafaring that largely sustained his culture and that functions as a metaphor for almost any activity in it, on land or on water. Every aspect from taxonomy to mythology is included. Similarly, each of the thirteen parts of the Messiaen work exhaustively chronicles the calls, the habitat, and the ecosystem of a bird species, evoking the complete world of a delimited area over the entire work. Each part focuses in addition on a different region or province of France, so the deliberately all-encompassing geography typical of the epic is also in evidence.

Nothing about the imitative music seems at first to transcend physical depiction in Messiaen's elegant collection of bird pieces, grounded in the French tone-painting tradition of eighteenth-century keyboard works like those of Rameau and Couperin, but the odd, iconoclastic emphasis on the religious and mythic in Jonke's tribute owes its presence to Messiaen's ecstatic, visionary belief in bird songs as a manifestation of God's immanence. An ornithologist with scientific publications based on extensive field work, Messiaen was also a joyously mystical Catholic who consciously connected bird song with Saint Francis of Assisi long before he composed his opera *Saint François d'Assise*, first performed in 1983, the sixth scene of which enacts Saint Francis's sermon to the birds. The whole dynamic of Saint Francis and his iconography so pervades "Catalogue d'oiseaux" that any reader would have to surmise Jonke's familiarity with Messiaen's opera, and Jonke indeed was present at a performance of *Saint François d'Assise* given at the Salzburg Festival in 1992 (Kling Interview 2004).

The first part of Jonke's work is accordingly not just a neutral cataloguing of bird types but is also an invocation, a summoning of all the other birds by the nightingale. (The title of that part, "Song of the Nightingale," is the same as that of an early work by Stravinsky, allowing Jonke to sneak in a subsidiary tribute.) The nightingale never says why he (she?) is gathering the other birds, but Jonke's oblique, persistent anthropomorphism ("wide-beak bespectacled shrikes and blue-headed organists . . . church finches, great broad-billed cardinals") anticipates the addresses to the human race delivered by a chorus of birds in parts two and four. Jonke is employing the reverse process of Messiaen in *Saint François d'Assise* by giving human attributes to birds, while the composer associates his main characters motivically with various bird calls (Messiaen 16). The other four parts reveal that the birds were in fact summoned, reversing the famous iconographic presentations of Saint Francis by Giotto and others, to deliver a two-part sermon (parts two and four) to humans. Between the two parts of the sermon is a second litany, one that exhibits to the full Jonke's gift for pertinent virtuosic parody. The fifth and last part is the apotheosis, the redeeming vision of happiness and peace beyond time–but only if the human race heeds the birds' sermon. Taken together, parts two through five, after the classic invocation, constitute a comprehensive "epic" of salvation history from the beginning of all things ("Humans! / We were here long before you") to the eschatological ending, the restoration of the golden age through universal harmony.

Part one is a kind of prologue, the verbal equivalent of a musical fantasia and a roll call by type and kind, in the form of a litany speeded to a canter by its prevalent dactylic meter. As so often with Jonke, pure invention seamlessly joins with objective observation to throw reality into doubt. Some of the most apparently outrageous names for birds are ornithologically accurate, while others are high-flying fabrications. The reader may choose to do research so as to determine which birds are in which category, but the more productive artistic response is probably to take a deep breath and enter the higher but zanier reality of Jonke's rhythmically hypnotic enumeration.

The middle three parts of "Catalogue d'oiseaux" portray respectively creation, redemption, and humanity's striving toward wholeness in comic modes that only Jonke could think up, giving in succession daft, madcap twists to Greek myth via religion, Christian salvation narrative, and Greek myth via philosophy. Each of these middle parts occupies a mythic dimension, then, addressing modes of piety and faith with a humor that only reinforces Jonke's esteem for the mystical aspect of Messiaen's art.

In the second part, "Chorus of Birds to the Human Race," the birds assert their claim to become once more the rightful gods of humanity, because they emerged at the beginning of time, after Zeus killed Kronos, to mark time from its very inception by the beating of their wings. Diametrically reversing Saint Francis's explanation to the birds about their nature in the scheme of God's loving creation, their fertility, their gift of song, their love of sunlight, and their immortal destiny in an eschatologically remade universe (Messiaen 23-5), the birds explain the origins of time in darkness and struggle, the sterility of Kronos's cyclical gestation and devouring of his children, the violence required to overthrow him, and their own superior status toward humans arising out of that scheme of creation. The birds do not preach to the human race about love, since such a thing does not seem to exist here, but about deference, power, and subservience, about order and degree. They do not comfort; they demand. All the terms of the Judeo-Christian creation narrative are parodistically negated through a grim vision, based on Greek mythology, of linear time emerging through violent action from a cycle of selfish destruction. One of the marks of parody is the unsettling combination of hilarity and gruesomeness pervading this section and others.

Jonke's gift of parody comes even more fully into its own in the third and central part, "The Sap-Sucking Woodpecker's Litany of Sacrifice," because it handles the core belief of Christianity, the salvific action of Jesus Christ, by combining clownish overexaggeration, the typical *multiplicatio ad absurdum*, with calculated bawdry. It is another equivalent of the exhaustively minute catalogues of ships, weapons, flora and fauna of the Homeric epics. Through sheer prolifieration of item after item,

Jonke reduces the sacrifice of the Cross to an absurdity that swamps all seriousness only to reinforce it while showing respect by inviting the kind of radical reconsideration that parody compels. Rather than view the emergence of the world as a deliberate act of creation, Jonke makes the first element of his parody the assumption that the whole cosmos came about by accident, something God did not want. And if it is already a stretch—a believer would call it a mystery—to see the death of Jesus Christ as a propitiatory act on behalf of all humanity, Jonke (or some human male, who at one point joins his voice to that of the sap-sucking woodpecker) stretches that act into Jesus's need to return again and again, as an amoeba, a clothes wardrobe, a crab louse, an ant, and of course a sap-sucking woodpecker, until all of creation is redeemed. But Jesus is at present trapped in a flask in some scientist's lab, since he has come back as a case of hay fever, so he needs redemption by the birds in order to be able to hatch as a divine dove, thus completing the creating, saving, and inspiring action of the Trinity.

Parody is not irreverence here. On the contrary, it is the necessary balance to reverence, just as doubt is the necessary accompaniment to faith. That multiplication of Jesus's redeeming act by becoming a member of every category whatever is at first absurd, since even a god/man could never, at least not in time, become one of everything animate and inanimate that had ever existed. But at the core of this mad multiplication is Saint Francis's vision of universal redemption, with nothing too humble for inclusion—"Toute chose de beauté doit parvenir à la liberté, la liberté de gloire. Nos frères oiseaux attendent ce jour . . . Ce jour où le Christ réunira toutes les créatures: celles de la terre, et celles du ciel!" (Messiaen 25). There are no limits in Saint Francis's view, because everything that exists, having been made by God, is intrinsically a thing of beauty or potentially capable of redemption into that state. If there is any basis at all for belief in the Biblical creation story, at the end of which God judged everything he had made as good (Genesis 1:31), then there must be room for the ameobas, the ants, the crab lice, and all the rest, however outlandish the idea may at first seem. Jonke has again reversed the terms of Christian belief in the salvation of the whole universe to set up a valid counterbalance to the usual clichés of worship and adoration.

The graphic vulgarity and bawdry of the sexual references in this section thus represent a calculated profanation, a category which in turn has no meaning without a religious sensibility. Jonke is once again using parody as a respectful tribute, avoiding sentimentality by violating taboos. There is no question of debunking for its own impudent sake, as in the superficially iconoclastic approach of a book like Lytton Strachey's *Eminent Victorians,* now itself painfully dated and sophomoric. Instead, Jonke is indulging what Mikhail Bakhtin, writing about Rabelais, calls the carnival humor, using " . . . lewd speech and gestures . . . " based on " . . . carnivalistic parodies of sacred texts and sayings" (49). Carnival endorses through blasphemy what it appears to be rejecting, for how could there be blasphemy except as a reaction to belief? It needs to be kept in mind, too, that this section is called a litany and that a litany is a prayer. Jonke's "carnival" parody does not arise from Christian belief on his part, however, but from respect for the epic worlds Messiaen created both as works of art and acts of faith, respect for dedication to beauty in any modality of ethics realized through aesthetics. Besides, religious reverence and carnival profanation aim equally at fertility, freedom, and fulfillment, and it is characteristic of Jonke to reveal the identity uniting apparent oppositions.

The fourth part, "Chorus of Birds to the Human Race II," reworks the speculations, themselves calculatedly droll to the point of parody, from Plato's *Symposium* about the way in which the two sexes were originally united, the birds again speaking, as in the second part, as if they had been eyewitnesses and are thus entitled to authority. The direct report by eyewitnesses of a state clearly existing only as mythic allegory is what gives this section its amusing tone, complete with testy rebukes by the birds about "the unbearable noise of your shrieks during copulation . . . ." The carnival tone of sensual indulgence is never quite absent in the three middle sections of "Catalogue d'oiseaux," but this fourth part is also a lament, an elegy for ingrained human loneliness and alienation that balances against parody to anticipate the restoration of a golden age, the reuniting of all things, in the last part.

The fifth part, the eschatology, restores peace, nullifies the power of objects to do harm, and ushers in the new millenium where death can have no dominion. It depicts a state of transcendent glory that goes past the need for Saint Francis's stigmata—the seventh scene of Messiaen's opera—since all suffering is annihilated in the achievement of the last things, with harmony restored and the wasting power of time annulled. Part two had shown time starting as the measure of Kronos's breathing, as a force born of maiming and attempted killing, but now time itself is redeemed by being brought to an end, no longer able to destroy or to record destruction. Messiaen wrote an early chamber work called "Quartet for the End of Time" (1940), and he took the redemption of time entirely for granted as part of the reunion of all creation eventually to be effected by Jesus at the end of the world. Again, part five strikes a complex balance, negotiating a border between the rhapsody of eschatological redemption and the buffoonery of its application to incongruously mundane objects and actions. Here, as throughout "Catalogue d'oiseaux," Jonke exhibits exuberance and energy of style, variety of rhythmic effect, and delight in life-giving proliferation, paying a tribute that does full justice to Messiaen's unmistakable elan.

The main problem facing anyone who writes about Beethoven is to demythologize an artist who has always been approached as if he were on a higher plane of humanity than any other composer or almost any other person whatever. Both Francis of Assisi and Beethoven were figures of myth and legend within their own lifetimes, but there is a wide fundamental difference in those myths. Francis's curing of the leper through a kiss; his calming of the ravening wolf; his sermon to the birds; his rapturous Canticle of the Sun; his initiating the devotion of the Christmas creche; his reception of the stigmata—these legends may be always ready to topple over into pure kitsch, always perilously subject to sentimental exploitation, but they emphasize a gentleness, a vulnerability, a purity of soul, a complete acceptance, and a readiness to find joy in suffering that make Francis almost uniquely beloved, even among nonbelievers. Has less bad ever been said about anyone? Francis's very way of being offers a gentle corrective to greed and violence, so it is no wonder that a composer who was not suffused with religious belief, Paul Hindemith, would have turned to him as the main figure of a ballet, *Nobilissima visione* (and note the title), during the threats and upheavals of the 1930s or that Messiaen, very much a believer, would have proposed the life of Francis as if to balance the narcissism and the indulgence of the 1970s and 1980s. *Saint François d'Assise* clearly has an impact on its audiences, too, because while they pointedly register its pageant-like stasis, its non-dramatic or even anti-dramatic quality, and its extreme length of almost six hours, they are enthusiastic, even enthralled, wherever they experience actual performance (Messiaen 16-7).

From the start, Beethoven's legends placed him at the opposite emotional pole from that of Francis and had him bestriding the narrow world like a colossus. He was made into the high-culture equivalent of a superhero from comic books and cartoons. Who could measure up to or feel comfortable with a musical titan who wrote works undreamed of in length and complexity, shaking the understanding of even his strongest admirers and railing at players and singers who said the works could not be performed as written? He was the fearless revolutionary politically engaged through his music, crossing out the dedication of his "Eroica" symphony on learning that Napoleon was to be crowned emperor, defying censorship through the passionate choruses for political freedom and the punishment of tyranny in his opera *Fidelio*. He was the fearless individualist who scorned all conformity with polite manners and all concessions to standard social forms, telling off influential patrons and unleashing tirades on his publishers, as he does on Schindler here. (Jonke depicts Handel as handling his own bid for autonomy more diplomatically and thus more successfully.) He was the suffering genius driven to near madness by being deprived of love and family, tortured by unbearable, superhuman loneliness and isolation made worse through his deafness, cut off from enriching human contact, losing his "Immortal Beloved" and the woman to whom he addressed the heartbreaking, anguished Heiligenstadt Testament. (The French respectfully but nervously call Beethoven "le grand sourd.") Finally, he was a mighty force of nature itself, legendarily shaking his fist at the sky during a thunderstorm on his deathbed. He is a figure of overpowering superlatives, not a man to whom anyone could humanly relate, and his musical successors, composers like Schumann and Brahms, were so daunted by trying to follow in his artistic footsteps that they wondered whether he had perhaps brought the symphony, the string quartet, and the piano sonata to such peaks of achievement that the forms themselves were essentially exhausted, much as Messiaen for years resisted Rolf Liebermann's plea to write an opera, convinced that " . . . there was no further scope for opera" (Messiaen 15) after Alban Berg's *Wozzeck* (1925), in turn a minor but important structural and thematic element in *Blinding Moment*.

Jonke goes about his task of humanizing Beethoven not by removing the nearly superhuman element, which is there from the start, but by balancing it against a nearly buffoonish nature and a pettiness not often emphasized in treatments of the composer. Beethoven scans the newspapers for booksellers' notices about the latest editions of Leibniz, but he is also an embryonic child of the consumerist age, interested to note all the advertising for the latest technologies, both in his field of music and otherwise. Rather than make Beethoven a larger-than-life mad genius, the wild-haired artist shouting and pounding his head against the wall to keep the rhythm while composing, Jonke shows him as something of a crank and a hypochondriac, or even a crackpot whose behavior is so strange—at least as reported by Schindler and validated by Beethoven—that the police in Wiener Neustadt would clearly have been derelict if they had *not* arrested him. It is natural for him to be interested in any device that might help him hear again, but he takes his crazy gadgets, his wild schemes, his treatments and prescriptions to near-obsessive extremes. Schindler's rebukes are not wrong because they have no foundation in reality, but only because they are self-serving. He is right in his warnings about Beethoven's need to exercise care, for the composer's normal base-line behavior is so eccentric that he escapes arrest in his familiar surroundings only because people are used to him. Beethoven certainly deserves sympathy as a victim of lesser and greater ailments, but his concern with doctors and ear machines becomes tedious. The scene in which he plays the tenth variation from the *Diabelli Variations* while wearing a huge headdress with two enormous protruding ear trumpets meant to help him bring the music to outward expression shows him as an unintentionally grotesque combination of crowned head and clown, one whose appearance on stage could indeed only be disruptive.

Most persons can no more relate to a fool than they can to a titan, however, especially when those aspects are present in the same measure at the same time, so Jonke develops Beethoven further as a simple vulnerable mortal, a person with ordinary needs common to all people. Though Beethoven takes a radical, high-handed position about being beholden to no other human being in a social contract, he needs and wants human conviviality. Once his rage can be seen as essentially a gentle rage, readers and theater audiences can identify with him in the time-honored Aristotelian manner of recognizing themselves in the main character of a play. Accordingly, while Beethoven needs time to himself, he is also glad of sympathetic human company and clearly relishes his time with Waldmüller. He is as winsomely pleased as a child to hear that he behaved well during the sittings for his portrait. He is eager to expend affection on his nephew and angry that he is prevented from doing so. Far from being the lonely creator in his ivory tower, he is consistently seeking opportunities to perform his music before audiences, even though he knows they might be baffled, and his concern with devices and gadgets to help him hear is in the service of his communicating with other humans to the fullest extent as man and artist, after all. Mundane concerns like finances plague him as much as they do anyone else, and while he can chide the servants, clearly aware of their cheating, he also feels compassionate toward them and others.

Only after Jonke has deftly performed this task of showing the great mythical Romantic hero of defiance and revolution to be a vulnerable mortal can the viewer identify with Beethoven to the point where his triumph, his apotheosis, and his glory take on understandable dimensions within a framework of human achievement. And since *Gentle Rage* is a stage work, Beethoven's triumph can be depicted in directly visible terms, as light radiates outward from the music being played, a motif always associated with godlike levels of creative power, as we saw with Handel, and a process of transformation or purification anticipated at the very beginning in Beethoven's comments about creatures turning into ever more translucent and rarified versions of their grosser selves through a kind of alchemical refinement.

Just as Beethoven had at his disposal a technically advanced piano on which he could expand the means of expression through the mighty *Hammerklavier* sonata, Opus 106 (named after the kind of piano on which it was to be performed), so *Gentle Rage* was commissioned by a Viennese piano manufacturer as a display piece for a new computerized instrument it was introducing. Because the *Hammerklavier* sonata and, at one point, one of the *Diabelli Variations*, opus 120, can sound on their own from the programmed piano, live but with no player at the keyboard, the audience is free to imagine the music as emerging from Beethoven's head, as if the viewer were present at the act of creation in process. But if the play closes with Beethoven sitting alone in his room and "thinking" the fugue from Opus 106, experiencing an elevation to pure light, as if he were being transformed into the most ethereal rendering of himself, the dramatic form reminds us that this action is in fact taking place the whole time in front of an audience. Beethoven retains a connection to the world in this way, even in his transformation, becoming more human as he becomes more godlike, for he is not content to be the solitary genius of Romantic myth, the Olympian splendidly isolated on his mountaintop. He needs to perform before an audience, but Schindler, thinking only of himself, had tried to thwart that need by mocking Beethoven's technical skill and implying that he would only alienate listeners through his bizarre antics. It turns out, however, that Beethoven knows at every moment exactly what he is doing and is willing to make a fool of himself in the service of a genuine, immediate artistic encounter with his audience.

What we could call the three sides of Beethoven's personality—the buffoonish, the vulnerable, and the godlike—are interwoven throughout *Gentle Rage*, and that balance enables the loftier aspects of Beethoven's life and work to emerge in a holistic human context. Beethoven is able to undergo purification into apotheosis because he is a human being, not a superhero, a man, not a god, for gods do not have to be accorded a godlike status they already have. His very first words, "My kingdom is in the air," are inevitably reminiscent of John 18:36, "My kingdom is not of this world," and he follows up at once with "I am what is," an echo of Exodus 3:14, "I am who am." He seems to be assuming the identity first of Jesus Christ and then of God the Father, a proud enough claim, but context shows that instead of overstepping his humanity he has subsumed it into a godlike task. He is the creator accepting the demands of his art and willing to suffer to bring it about as he brings the *Hammerklavier* sonata and the *Diabelli Variations* to fulfillment. By the end of the play, Beethoven has attained that status of enacting *logos* that we noted in Handel and that is the ideal of every creative artist. The composer is now breathing not just air, but also light, so the room is growing darker. But when the light is created again, in replication of divine fiat, it comes through the music, not through the person of the artist. Beethoven is the bringer of a light he knows he has conveyed but did not originate.

The radiant fulfillment that marks the end of all four pieces in this collection never means that freedom from suffering or release from the contingent woes of mortality has been achieved. Suffering can grow more intense as a function of the transformation to a higher plane, for that matter. Handel is blind and paralyzed, more exhausted and feeble than ever; Webern finds the closing chord of his musical life in the three notes Raymond Bell plays him, but those "notes" are the three shots that kill him; Francis of Assisi achieves even greater spiritual stature by embracing his literal vulnerability in accepting the pain of the stigmata, while, in the eschatological scheme of "Catalogue d'oiseaux," the transcendence at the end of time is promise, a vision, not an achieved reality, with humanity still seeking its fulfillment through the reuniting of the sexes. And in addition to his other burdens, Beethoven can be seen by a set of passing allusions toward the end of *Gentle Rage* as a man grieving over his loneliness more deeply than ever. He wants to become his nephew's legal guardian (and in actual life did become so for a time), but the terms in which he speaks of escaping with the boy to England and his hostility toward the boy's mother suggest a variation on the configuration of Claudius, Gertrude, and Hamlet, an archetypal tragedy of mother and son, uncle and nephew in which all sorts of displaced loyalties and dark treacheries tear apart the characters, in which the supposed freedom of Hamlet's journey to England was planned as a journey to death. Beethoven calls his nephew's mother the Queen of the Night, the power-driven, scheming villainess and mother of Pamina in Mozart's *The Magic Flute*, who would rather see her daughter dead than out of her control. Beethoven is the God of Moses, the suffering servant of Isaiah, the creator participating in the divine work of *logos*, but he is also the haunted, lost Hamlet of his own tragic family drama, a sad man lost in malice and sorrow.

Just as Handel goes blind toward the end of his life and sees with his ears, so Beethoven learns to hear with his eyes, a process that began during his youth when his sight was engaged in both seeing and hearing himself at a great distance and then seeing and hearing that self in turn apprehending the first watcher. Synesthesia, the bewilderment of perception by the displacement of one sense function to another, becomes for Beethoven, as it does for Handel, a kind of higher awareness, not a confusing muddle. And if the watcher can watch the watcher in infinite regress, like mirrored images of mirrored images, then this potentially disorienting *mise en abîme*, likely to confound most persons' hold on reality, becomes a means of heightened awareness for Beethoven, giving him additional resources to overcome impairment. Likewise, Webern experiences in *Blinding Moment* the same infinite replication of himself in Prague watching himself in Vienna watching himself in Prague, back and forth ad infinitum, but the moment of extreme geographical displacement is also the moment when Webern experiences his clearest insight into his need to leave Prague and go back to Vienna at once. What looks like a ceaseless and pointless oscillation between the two cities is in fact a classic turning point of preliminary resolution for Webern.

More than one critic has called the novella *Blinding Moment* Jonke's masterpiece, one of his most finely and intricately wrought fictions (Amann "Des Unsagbaren Nachtgesang" 52), perhaps because Jonke worked and reworked the material even more often than was customary with him. It began as a radio play on which Jonke collaborated, was expanded as a television film in 1986, appeared as a printed script in the journal *manuskripte* in 1987, and was then published as a novella in 1996 in *Stoffgewitter* 94-159 (Hemecker 301). The commission for the new film was Jonke's reward for saving the Handel project. He was given carte blanche as a gesture of gratitude, and his earlier training in film and television at the Academy for Music and the Performing Arts in Vienna equipped him with the practical knowledge and skills to participate actively in every phase of production. In fact, Jonke himself was given complete control after a break with the director, Michael Mrakitsch, who was bent on portraying the politically naïve and uninvolved Webern as a consciously committed National Socialist (Hengstler 234-5). Aside from directing the remaining scenes, Jonke chose all the music on the sound track and coordinated it with the images; when Webern is on a mountaintop, high above a glacier, for instance, Jonke intensifies the floating or soaring visual effect by choosing Webern's op. 2, the cantata "Entflieht auf leichten Kähnen," with its tonal system that the composer himself called "schwebend" or "soaring" (Angerer 186). Even more intensely than in the Handel piece, then, the novella version of this material shows unusually clear traces

of its visual source, and the novella is at times almost inter-
changeable with the film in its graphic sharpness.

Jonke is meticulous in specifying genre. He calls *Gentle Rage*
a "theater sonata," drawing attention to a motivic structure that
emphasizes the combination of the zany, the vulnerably mortal,
and the godlike in Beethoven. That technique of constantly developing and transmuting those motifs carries the dynamic of the
play more than any standard plot line. It is worth observing,
then, that Jonke designated his final version of *Blinding Moment*
a "novella," in which connection Hemecker (301) astutely recalls
Goethe's point that a novella must be organized around a "novum." In Goethe's memorable phrase, every novella has at its
core "eine unerhörte Begebenheit," an amazing, unexpected inci-
dent as the heart of the action. Jonke fulfills that dictate of genre
in two ways, once in content and once in structure. For the first,
would it be possible to make up a story more bizarre than the
facts of Webern's death? He and his wife had moved from Vienna
to Mittersill, near Salzburg, in February 1945, after the death of
their son, to get away from the advancing Russian front and to be
near their daughters and grandchildren. Out of consideration for
the children, Webern stepped outside his one daughter's house at
around 9:00 P.M. on September 15 to smoke a cigar in the open
air, not knowing that it was under observation by the American
army for suspected black market activity. The army had given
notice that curfew violators were subject to being shot without
warning, and the instant Raymond Bell, one of the soldiers on
patrol—and himself apparently involved in the black market—saw
the flame from the match, he fired three times, killing Webern
instantly.

The novella is as dense and complex as the film, which blends
"the genres of historical film, dramatized documentary, film
about an artist or musician, film noir, and psychological thriller"
(Hengstler 237) but, again like the film, never loses sight of the
central episode, the death of Webern and its enduring effects on
his killer. Jonke says that his imagination was triggered not so
much by the strangeness of the killing itself, however astonish-
ing, as by his discovering that Raymond Bell died of alcoholism
exactly ten years to the day after his victim (Kling Interview
2002). The structure of the entire work emerges from this juxtaposition of the two men, the balanced opposition and constant
interplay of their similarities and differences, beginning with a

headnote set off typographically and italicized at the opening of the story: *"In September 1945 Dr. Anton Webern was shot by U.S. Army cook R. N. Bell, who died in September 1955."* As Jonke expressed it in an interview, the same blinding moment, the flash of the match and the bullets, was common to both men, though "it took one of them about ten seconds (or less) to die, the other ten years" (Kling Interview 2002). The consistent technique of juxtaposition forms the second "novum," an unusual but thematically appropriate method of structural development. Jonke uses strategic repetition, imitating Webern's buildup of structure through small cells of canonic motifs. Just as Webern orchestrated J. S. Bach's "Ricercare" from the *Musical Offering* to draw emphasis away from linear structure and toward separate pointillist tone colors, so Jonke moves his novella away from linear chronology by isolating different individual points along a set of coordinates, the x axis Webern's life up to the moment of the shooting and the y axis Raymond Bell's life from the moment of the shooting until his death ten years later.

The narrator travels back and forth in time along this set of coordinates with the shooting, the fatal blinding moment, as their point of intersection. This omniscient and omnipresent narrator addresses the whole story by turns to Bell, using the familiar form "Du," and to Webern, using the formal "Sie," in that way avoiding the misplaced subjectivity of first-person narration and the false objectivity of third-person (Hemecker 302). Bell's story moves mostly forward in time, from the shooting to his terrible death from delirium tremens a decade later, while Webern's moves mainly backward, from the moment of death to the beginning of his musical career. The narrator is equally at home with both characters, so readily able to switch from one axis of the coordinates to the other as to show him free from space as well as time, and his comprehensive approach further serves to establish a range of entirely unsuspected spiritual kinships between killer and victim. Jonke depicts Bell as of course never realizing who Webern was or why he was notable, just as Webern could never have known anything about Bell. Yet the very strangeness, the improbability of their chance convergence, is the basis on which the narrator builds his exploration of two lives much more alike than they would ever appear on the surface. Jonke's theme of contingent, vulnerable mortality unites all people.

A narrator who can freely move beyond time and space in this way is witnessing the events in the lives of both men *sub specie æternitatis*, from a standpoint of eternity, from which he is able to explore possible alternatives to what in fact irreversibly happened in a split second within time and space. He can accordingly "advise" Webern and Bell about what they might do differently to prevent the catastrophe. Right from the beginning, this narrator urges Bell to be less jumpy, to give himself time to think before he shoots, and at the end, he admonishes Bell to relax, take a deep breath, and to count off a few seconds, while he cautions Webern to smoke inside. "No, your wife doesn't mind . . . and why not show your grandchildren . . . how to blow smoke rings from your mouth." His process is not an attempt to change history in a facile, "what-if" science-fiction way, especially since adopting any of the alternatives the narrator urges is never offered as even a remote possibility. Instead, the narrator's freedom from linearity in time and space gives him a chance to observe and comment, but without being able to change anything. His freedom only makes him and his readers more aware of how contingent the shooting was, of how contingent every moment of any human encounter is. The narrator's method leads him to acknowledge transience and frailty rather than override them, and it is in that acknowledgment that *Blinding Moment* achieves the greatness of profound pity, because the same narrator who is omniscient and omnipresent holds to the awareness that he is not omnipotent. He accepts that he cannot change anything, since the moment of Webern's and Bell's convergence was the moment of death for both; Webern's of course, but Bell was already hopelessly far gone in alcoholism, and his remorse over shooting Webern only seals a doom inevitable long before.

Hemecker calls Jonke's narrator "Olympian" (302), but the narrative perspective ironically underscores the utter inability of the narrator to intervene in events. He can be in the minds of the two men, he can retell them their own lives as they are dying, in the classic manner of one's whole life passing in review at the moment of death, he can know them even better than they know themselves, he can unite them and mesh their fates, plotting more points of coordination along axes of whose design they themselves are unaware, but he willingly, if with heavy heart, accepts the human limitations of the time and space outside which he stands. If the narrator is the creator, the arranger of the story, he can emulate the work of God but not be God himself, a theme that occurs constantly in these pieces and throughout Jonke's work. The narrator has the humility that comes of knowing his own limits and those of all humans, of realizing that life is more tentative than we often dare think. His knowledge in turn lends him a compassion that marks all the protagonists in Jonke who decline to arrogate to themselves godlike qualities that no mortal can possess. Like Joyce's *Ulysses*, *Blinding Moment* combines ingenuity of experiment in narrative structure with compassionate portrayal of human loss and suffering.

Or, better for Jonke's context, like Georg Büchner's play of profound moral compassion, *Woyzeck*, made into the opera *Wozzeck* by Alban Berg (1925), a close friend of Webern's and, with him, the main pupil of Arnold Schoenberg. Accordingly, Bell is Wozzeck or Woyzeck (Büchner's first editor misread a *y* for a *z*), a common soldier victimized by the brutality of war and by power structures that threaten dehumanization. While Büchner's play elevates to the level of heartrending terror and pity a semi-deranged, incoherent soldier who kills the woman he lives with, Berg's *Wozzeck* deepens further yet the viewer's anguish over the fate of an inarticulate man driven to violence. The opera is one of the great achievements of musical drama, a shattering portrayal of doomed individual fates and a pitying but ferocious indictment of social callousness and cruelty, an achievement so great it is no wonder that Messiaen doubted whether opera was a possible form of art after it. Against the backdrop of *Wozzeck*, the narrator's address to Bell is charged with poignancy and compassion:

> Where are you, Raymond, don't hide, one of the Herr Doctor's [Webern's] friends over there is writing a whole opera about you, over on the other side, it's called *Wozzeck*, only you have the advantage that you don't have to stab your wife, you got rid of her so you could drink in peace, or let the Atlantic drink you, you just wait for the surging billows to swallow you . . . .

The narrator compares Bell with the pitiable Wozzeck, even using when speaking to Bell the same phrases Wozzeck uses in the play and the opera to try expressing his sense of justice. More outside of time than inside, where our view is too limited, the connection of all humans through suffering, especially through mortality, can be observed. The narrator makes parallels not only between Bell and Webern, but he places the hapless killer in relation to Berg as well on the basis of their common mortality. " . . . things are bad over there in Europe, too, Raymond, the bad times will soon be back . . . but you could easily visit Alban Berg and thank him, before he dies, which will be soon, for his opera about you, about somebody like you."

The connection with Berg also focuses the narrator's compassion, not to say tenderness, for Webern's fate, and long before the moment of the shooting. Webern, so dauntingly austere in personality and forbiddingly arcane in technique, is shown here as a musician forced all his professional life to undergo "isolation . . . sacrifice, humiliation" for his art, a frail genius whose sufferings culminate in a kind of protracted nervous breakdown he suffers after the freakish death of Berg at age 50 in 1935 (blood poisoning from an untreated insect bite). Berg died just after finishing his violin concerto, itself a memorial to a young friend who had died of meningitis, and Webern was asked to conduct the premiere in Barcelona in 1936.

It is a matter of historical fact that Webern withdrew after a number of disastrous rehearsals, and the usual explanation is that his conducting ability was unequal to the task. Jonke seizes on that implausible reason here. Webern had long been a successful conductor of works more complex than the Berg Violin Concerto (Lasinger 3-17), after all, famously performing Mahler's symphonies with musicians who could not even read music, so inexperience or ineptitude would hardly have been the real reason. Instead, as Jonke's narrator keeps intimating, Webern's inability to get beyond the opening few chords of the concerto in rehearsal arises from a crippling perfectionism rooted in his inability to come to terms with Berg's death. Again and again, for page after page of *Blinding Moment*, Webern demands a sound from the orchestra that it cannot give –"the sound has to be present before you play it"–and he starts over and over until the narrator suggests, "No, Herr Doctor, there's nothing you can do, break it off at once," whereupon Webern tells the orchestra that nothing can ever be definitively brought to completion and walks out. The narrator has unlimited insight into the characters and zero influence on them. He sees where Webern's emotional state is leading him, knows that his paralysis and rage are not a matter of musical standards any longer but a baffled sidewards expression of a grief he cannot get over.

Likewise, Bell is haunted for the rest of his life by a silence from which he knows will always emerge, in his obsessive reliving of it, the sound of the three shots and the voice of Webern asking, "Why did you shoot me?" The question demands an answer, and all the way to the end, up to the moment of his own death, Bell imagines himself being able to say truthfully, "I didn't," tortured all the more by being exonerated after a token fourteen days of confinement to quarters right after the fatal event. The soldier's homecoming, the restoration to harmony, will never be real to Bell, because he will never stop reenacting the blinding moment. Out of pity, the narrator says to him quite often, "Just wait a few seconds," knowing it is too late. Webern has no reason to feel responsible for Berg's death, but he is temporarily broken by it anyway; a close friend and fellow musician is no more. Bell is the direct cause of Webern's death, and permanent regret and remorse destroy him; it does not matter that he never knew Webern and had no idea who he was. On the plane of eternity, differences of every sort yield to the universal, elemental human fate out of which arise the pity and terror of tragedy, the compassion of catharsis, even when, as in this novella, the catharsis cannot involve a change of direction.

Webern and Bell are similar in the universality of their mortal state, then, and different in the particulars of their individual lives. The settings work in *Blinding Moment* to unify these opposite movements. By its nature as a system of coordinates, the structure traces divergence and convergence at the same time, shown above all by the physical placement of the characters. Both Bell and Webern are seen walking along dark corridors, for example, telling themselves, or being told by the narrator, to be careful. In a futile hope of staving off the inevitable, Webern is shown almost endlessly walking along the corridor in his daughter's house that leads to the outside door, while Bell is wandering the corridors of some fantasy-like building of his own mind, one that leads to the moment when he will shoot his victim. (The effect is even more pronounced in the film, where the severely impaired Bell is living his last days in a long-abandoned hotel and ceaselessly trudging the corridors.) As for the differences, the coordinates are extended or truncated in length. Webern is depicted as a mountain climber, scaling greater and greater heights through his wanderings, while Bell lives progressively closer to the ground, ending up on a mattress on the floor in the old hotel, falling off even this elevation and finally lying directly on the sidewalk (as depicted in the film). At the heights and the depths alike dwells the poignancy that unites all people.

Comedy covers a wide range of modes. As noted earlier, it need have nothing to do with merriment or laughter, and humor is conspicuous by its absence from *Blinding Moment*. The emergence of light, which means creative energy and renewed life in the other pieces here, is the flash of death for Webern and the final doom for Bell. Yet Webern unreservedly understands and accepts that the shots fired by Bell are the fit punctuation closing his life as an artist. Not only does he have no regret, but he sees Bell as the illuminator of his own art. Addressing his killer, he says,

> ... you enjoyed the great success of producing with absolute accuracy and at the precise pitch and volume stipulated in the score the final three notes you played during the last piece—with your threefold shots and the loud reports, the explosive banging sounds directed at my person, you enabled me . . . to draw to a conclusion most credible to all the world, made it possible for me simply to bring to an end, signaling its closure by way of a musically perfect culminating chord, the finale of my life, a life made up of musical sounds . . . .

Death comes to everyone, if not ordinarily as abruptly, freakishly, and violently as it did to Webern. What scheme of religious or philosphical illumination, what mode of spirituality, what way of pursuing wisdom counsels the seeker to ignore death? Instead, the embrace of mortality represents a great attainment of the soul and a profound human resolution. Webern is therefore not a tragic character in the grotesque mode of his death but a comic one in the generosity with which he greets his fate and thanks Bell for giving his life its highest meaning. No more than most other work by Jonke is *Blinding Moment* conventional comedy, but Jonke is not a conventional writer.

Works Cited

Alewyn, Richard. "Der Tod des Ästheten." Über Hugo von Hofmannsthal (1958). 4th ed. Göttingen, Vandenhoeck & Ruprecht, 1967. 64-77.

Amann, Klaus. "Des Unsagbaren Nachtgesang." In *Die Zeit* 22 Nov. 1996: 52.

Amann, Klaus. "Literaturlandschaft Kärnten." Kaukoreit and Pfoser 205-08.

Angerer, Manfred. "Weberns Opera 1 bis 31." In Hilmar 185-204.

Bakhtin, Mikhail. *Literatur und Karneval: Zur Romantheorie und Lachkultur.* Munich: Hanser, 1969.

Bartens, Daniela and Paul Pechmann, eds. *Gert Jonke.* Dossier: Die Buchreihe über österreichische Autoren 11. Graz: Droschl, 1996.

Friedl, Harald, ed. *Die Tiefe der Tinte.* Salzburg: Verlag Grauwerte im Institut für Alltagskultur, 1990.

Gamper, Herbert. "Die Wörter und das Schweigen: Zum Werk Gert Jonkes." *Die Zeit und die Schrift: Österreichische Literatur nach 1945.* Ed. Karlheinz F. Auckenthaler. Acta germanica 4. Szeged: Jate, 1993. 159-69.

Handke, Peter. "In Sätzen steckt Obrigkeit." In Bartens and Pechmann 251-5.

Hemecker, Wilhelm. "Gert Jonkes 'Geblendeter Augenblick': Eine Annäherung. *Modern Austrian Literature* 31 (1998): 301-307.

Hilmar, Ernst, ed. *Anton Webern 1883-1945: Anton Webern zum hundertsten Geburtstag.* Intro. Henri Pousseur. Vienna: Universal, 1983.

Jonke, Gert. "Caryatids and Atlantes—Vienna's First Guest Workers." Trans. Vincent Kling. *Review of Contemporary Fiction*, 35: 1 (2005), 67-79.

---. "Catalogue d'oiseaux." *kolik* 20, 2002, 18-24.

---. "Danube River Bridge." Trans. Vincent Kling. *Review of Contemporary Fiction*, 35: 1 (2005), 65-7.

---. *Der Kopf des Georg Friedrich Händel*. Salzburg: Residenz, 1988.

---. *Erwachen zum großen Schlafkrieg: Erzählung*. Salzburg: Residenz, 1982.

---. *Geblendeter Augenblick. Stoffgewitter*. Salzburg: Residenz, 1996. 94-159.

---. *Geometric Regional Novel*. Trans. and afterword by Johannes Vazulik. Normal, IL: Dalkey Archive, 2000 (1994).

---. *Himmelstraße—Erdbrustplatz oder Das System von Wien*. Salzburg: Residenz, 1999.

---. *Sanftwut oder Der Ohrenmachinist: Eine Theatersonate*. Salzburg: Residenz, 1990.

---. *Schule der Geläufigkeit*. Frankfurt/Main: Suhrkamp, 1977.

---. *Stoffgewitter*. Salzburg: Residenz, 1996.

Kathrein, Karin. "Irrwitz und Komik und totale Schönheit." *Kurier* (Vienna). Special Issue—*Nestroy-Preis*. 15 Nov. 2003: 7.

Kaukoreit, Volker and Kristina Pfoser, eds. *Die österreichische Literatur seit 1945: Eine Annäherung in Bildern*. Stuttgart: Reclam, 2000.

Kling, Vincent. "Gert Jonke." *Review of Contemporary Fiction*, 35: 1 (2005), 7-63.

---. Personal Interview with Gert Jonke. Vienna, June and July, 2002 (several sessions).

---. Personal Interview with Gert Jonke. Vienna, June and July, 2004 (several sessions).

Lasinger, Margarethe, ed. *Anton von Webern-Fest: Ein Wochenende mit dem Œuvre von Anton von Webern* (Program Booklet of the Wiener Festwochen 2004.) Vienna: Wiener Festwochen, 2004.

Lux, Joachim, ed. *Gert Jonke:* Chorphantasie (Program Booklet.) Vienna: Burgtheater/Akademietheater 2003.

Menasse, Robert. "Die sozialpartnerschaftliche Ästhetik: Das Österreichische an der österreichischen Literatur der Zweiten Republik." *Überbau und Undergrund: Die sozialpartnerschaftliche Ästhetik: Essays zum österreichischen Geist.* (1990). Frankfurt: Surhkamp, 1997. 11-110.

Messiaen, Olivier. *Saint François d'Assise.* Opéra en 3 actes: tableaux 3, 6, 7, 8. Orfeo CD C 485 982 1. Salzburger Festspiele 1985. Conductor Lothar Zagrosek.

Rauchbauer, Otto and Monika Wittmann. "»Mordio—Feurio--Diebio«: Hilde Spiels kreative Leistung als Übersetzerin englischer Dramatik." In Hans A. Neunzig and Ingrid Schramm, eds., *Hilde Spiel: Weltbürgerin der Literatur. Profile: Magazin des österreichischen Literaturarchivs.* Band 3. Vienna: Zsolnay, 1999.

Reiterer, Reinhold. "Listiger Sprach-Anarchist." *Bühne: Österreichs Theater- und Kulturmagazin.* May 2003. 90-91.

Schmidt-Dengler, Wendelin. "Zu *Der Kopf des Georg Friedrich Händel.*" In Bartens and Pechmann 324-326.

Zweig, Stefan. "Georg Friedrich Händels Auferstehung." *Sternstunden der Menschheit: Zwölf historische Miniaturen.* Vienna: Büchergilde Gutenberg, 1951. 73-100.

Literary translators have it easier than writers generating a new text. Translation has daunting challenges, but one of them is not having to invent something that doesn't already exist. Even so, translators' problems never go away, so it's advisable for us to have all the friends we can get for the times of seeming failure. Meaning all the time, because translation by its nature must fail, must fall short. Thurber had a cartoon showing people standing around at a literary cocktail party and talking about an author who was trying to get his books translated into various foreign languages because they lost so much in the original. The certain loss is in the opposite direction, though, and inevitably. Think about it–the perfect translation could only be a rendering that captures every sound, rhythm, nuance, and structure of the original with complete fidelity, and that's impossible, because it would mean replicating the source text in every respect. The only really "faithful" translation of any literary work would be a clean photocopy of the original.

Martin A. Hainz faces the problem forthrightly in the opening comments of his outstanding collection on literary translation. As he explains–and I translate!–the phlogiston theory was disproved as an actual physical phenomenon centuries ago, but "it would seem that in literature *phlogiston* really does exist . . . because in every translation something gets lost that is as substantial as it is sublime" (2). Nobody ever tells translators that, and until they find it out the hard way, they feel guilty and inadequate for lapses that inhere in making the effort at all. Why else would they bother to respond when reviewers tax them with missing something, which is the same as saying that it gets dark when the sun goes down? Book-review publications are always featuring hurt and indignant "exchanges" full of "gotcha" accusations and huffy, injured rebuttals that waste everyone's time and energy by expanding on the self-evident. These exchanges would seem as pointless as they are if the editors of those publications would think to reprint the sensible observation of one great translator, Hilde Spiel, who wrote in 1970 to *her* editor, Heinrich M. Ledig-Rowohlt–and again I translate! –

> . . . translations are like those routines in which floor acrobats build human pyramids. It's easier to climb higher on the shoulders of others than to start off on the ground. What I mean is that every translation can be corrected, because someone else will always be able to think of a better, smoother turn of phrase. That's the advantage editors' readers have. The translator is stuck in his text and can't very easily find a way out. (qtd. in Rauchbauer 111)

Humbling words, because they mean in this case that any reader of the four Jonke pieces in this collection who knows even a little German is likely to find better phrases and expressions than the ones here. Such a reader might even find actual mistakes. But if being open to correction is good enough for Hilde Spiel, who made such fine translations into German of Edna O'Brien, Joe Orton, and Tom Stoppard, it's good enough for me.

Two more levels of discouragement cause a translator to need companions and friends. What about those great translations in which more seems to get added than lost? Some renderings are monuments of style, grace, accuracy, and pure beauty, as if the vanished phlogiston had been replaced with something even more essential and precious. If envy is in fact a deadly sin, I have no more chance of redemption in the next world than I do of perfection in this one. From Urquhart and Motteux's Rabelais to Natasha Wimmer's rendering of Roberto Bolaño's *The Savage Detectives*, really great translations are the joy and the despair of anyone working at the craft. A few peaks: Tobias Smollett's versions of Le Sage; C. K. Scott Moncrieff's Proust; H. T. Lowe-Porter's Thomas Mann; Eugene Jolas's version of Alfred Döblin's *Alexanderplatz Berlin*; Archibald Colquhoun's incredibly elegant translation of Lampedusa's incredibly elegant *The Leopard*; and Anthony Hecht's jaw-dropping versions of lyrics by Goethe and Baudelaire. Read them, then weep for sheer happiness and frustration. And there are astounding achievements from English, too, like Hilde Spiel's Stoppard, Hans Wollschläger's outstanding *Ulysses*, and Erich Fried's excellent renderings of Shakespeare's plays. Translators who savor work on this level and then compare these achievements to their own are likely to need shoulders to cry on.

Especially because there's one more level of frustration. Many a reader might get huffy about some of the translators praised here. After all, their work has been superseded by "translations for our time," to use a favorite buzz phrase. "Everybody knows" that Scott Moncrieff's work was inaccurate, overlyrical, too rhapsodic, "unfaithful," in a word. But unfaithful to whom or to what? Was Pope "unfaithful" to Homer? Errors by the hundreds were (allegedly) found in Moncrieff's *Remembrance of Things Past* (start with the title itself), but none of the clodhopping replacements comes within hailing distance of Moncrieff's irony, rhetorical balance, and witty, unobtrusive deployment of three or more tones at once. Of course *Sodom and Gomorrah* is more literal and accurate than *Cities of the Plain*, but the literal title comes out bumpkinish in English, and that's not by any means the worst example of Proust "for our time." "We're all aware" (aren't we?) that Lowe-Porter was lamentably Victorian, fustian, bombastic, doing great injustice to Mann—or could it be that she was mirroring with great skill, in a way that later translators apparently have no idea of, the majestic, slow, old-fashioned rhythms and tempos of Mann, who always looked at least one generation backward in his language, like W. G. Sebald after him? That doesn't mean any older translation is always better than any newer one. Edith Grossman's English version of *Don Quixote* compares with any that has gone before it, and it is a masterpiece in its own right, especially because it never tries "ye-olde" period language. Much too often, though, publishers and reviewers bad-mouth older translations for purely marketing purposes. Read reviews of some much-heralded "translation for our time," and you'll likely see that there's no specific analysis, no detailed reading, but only a set of general points about how wretched last year's translation is, how stiff and ungainly, compared to the suppleness and idiomatic perfection of the latest and greatest. Reviewers seem to be fed this stuff by publishers' press materials. The advertisers of new and improved laundry products are more honest, meantime, because they have no intellectual pretensions.

So with all this discontent, translators need not just *a* friend, but a bevy of them. I know how lucky I am to have them. In the first place, Gert Jonke has been generous and gracious from the day we met—completely by accident on the 2A bus line in Vienna, but that's another story. He never attempts to direct his commentators or translators, and his only hint to me, besides reminding me that words do have lexical meanings, was to emphasize the importance of the sound, of rhythm and pacing. That's not as hard as it might seem, either, because no matter how elaborate Jonke's language becomes, it is always grounded in the spoken language, like that of Henry James or William Faulkner. I have been especially guided by a statement Jonke made to Harald Friedl (109): ". . . no sooner do people hear me at a public presentation than they stop having difficulties reading my books, because they suddenly discern the rhythmic curve and get the hang of what's there." I take it as an axiom that all translators must clearly hear what they have written, and this process is at least as vital for Jonke as for any other writer. At any rate, his clear interest in what his translator produces, combined with his release into complete freedom, makes the collaboration memorable. I won't forget the smile on his face when I read him, at his request, the "Song of the Nightingale," part one of "Catalogue d'oiseaux," at a table in the Café Sperl one bleak winter afternoon at the end of 2005.

Though I know Jonke's publisher, Dr. Jochen Jung of Jung and Jung, Salzburg and Vienna, through brief correspondence only, I hail him for the support he so generously offers–first to writers, because he produces their new work and reprints their older titles in handsome volumes, beautifully designed and carefully edited; second to the work of translation in general, one witness to which is his attractive dual-language edition of Hart Crane's *The Bridge* in Ute Eisinger's fine German rendering, *Die Brücke*; third to me in particular, a translator unknown to him but one to whom he granted immediate blanket permission for this project and others involving Jonke. Dr. Jung's kind and forthcoming manner is matched by the same qualities in my own publisher, Jorun Johns of Ariadne Press, always ready to help, support, and encourage. My conversations in Klosterneuburg and Vienna with this gracious and cultivated lady have made me a more civilized person.

Friends and collaborators have sustained me both in Europe and in the United States. Johanna Sieber's keen curiosity about language, her patient interest as I struggle with particulars of phrasing and expression, her command of both German and English combine with her human warmth to earn my gratitude for this friendship. Andreas Fischbacher's cover for this book is

only the most obvious of his contributions that help and sustain
me with unfailing encouragement on every professional and personal level, and I am very thankful for having him as a friend and
a collaborator on this project. Erhan Altan, who translates Austrian experimental poetry into his native Turkish and actually
finds grants and publishers, has taught me more through his un-
quenchable passion and his practical knowledge than I ever
hoped to know; his guidance and support, his belief in the power
of cultural transmittal, his faith and courage are beyond my power of thanks. Over many years, Lara Pokorny has validated my
work and followed it with an informed, intelligent interest that
brings new motivation; what more could I ask than such a friend,
one who believes in me and what I am doing?

Friends and critics in Philadelphia are always ready to help
me test my ear by listening and commenting when I read aloud
and by offering suggestions for improvement as well as plaudits
when they're earned. Bruno Kreisky is said to have remarked,
"You have no idea how much praise I can stand." The friends I
name now give me all I need and then some, but the praise is dis-
criminating and informed, not automatic. John Lord has as keen
an eye as an ear; he often asks me to backtrack when I'm reading
aloud so he can grasp a rhythm or a structure, and his profes-
sional-level copy-editing skill has often saved me embarrass-
ment. Jason Ager and Joe Campbell are the kind of humanist
they don't make any more–passionate about the power of literature to change lives and always ready to share their honest in-
sights and criticisms of my work with me. Jeff Renye is quieter,
but his reflective, often silent listening tells me all I need to hear.
Focus is the hallmark of the engagement these friends offer, and
I happily reap all the benefit they confer.

The total support I can always count on from my family–my
sisters, their husbands, and their children–is beyond price, all
the more sustaining because it is not grounded in professional
knowledge but in sheer affection and acceptance. How do I give
thanks for a lifetime of family love at its best?

More than one institution has helped in ways without which I
could never undertake this work. In Vienna, the *"Literaturhaus,"*
officially the *Dokumentationsstelle für neuere österreichische Literatur,* has provided a quiet working atmosphere with helpful
support from staff members, especially Dr. Heinz Lunzer and Dr.
Anne Zauner. The staff of the literature archive of the Austrian

National Library, the *Literaturarchiv der österreichischen Nationalbibliothek*, has also been friendly, generous, and supportive, and I would like to thank especially Dr. Klaus Kastberger, Dr. Ingrid Schramm, and Mag. Martin Wedl for help on this project and others. In Philadelphia, my home institution has paid me, encouraged me, catalogued me, and provided me the structure I need to work. Not to forget the revitalizing involvement with so many students over so many years, I turn to supportive colleagues. Both my former chair, Dr. Patricia Haberstroh, and my current chair, Dr. Bernhardt Blumenthal, are constant in their encouragement. Bernie, always a yea-sayer to any worthwhile academic project, offers freedom and support, and I always feel his attitude sustaining me. It was Pat who "made" me apply for a Fulbright guest professorship to Vienna in 1996, and that appointment was the ratifying act in a lifelong love of Austrian literature, the end of the betrothal and the beginning of the marriage. That love makes the frustrations involved in translating a welcome burden. After all, if even one reader of this book comes to esteem Jonke, the trouble is worth it, and if not, the work is a joy for its own sake.

  Above all, I thank Professor Adolf D. Klarmann, that passionate advocate of Austrian studies (*"Ein Gedankenstrich von Franz Grillparzer ist wertvoller als ein ganzes Stück von Friedrich Hebbel!"*–a bit rhetorical, but it got my attention). More than giving me a professional direction, Klarmann believed in me long before I could believe in myself. It is a sorrow to have lost him years ago and a joy to dedicate this volume as a small memorial to him. May it be a quiet requiem and a small stone on his grave.